The Dragon Common Room collects and connects threads of history, literature, mythology, and art to craft stories with Christian symbolism that guide us and cast their light in us.

We are on a quest to resurrect the English language from the tomb of Modernity and its corporate and scientific jargon. We seek to revive this trade language with the heartbeat of poetry that has been discarded from the culture of the Anglophone World. Simply put: without poetry, our language dies. We're waking the dead.

COMING SOON: A FAËRIE TALE, FULLY-ILLUSTRATED, WITH DRAGONS

DRACO ALCHEMICUS is an epic fantasy in five acts. It's also a voyage to leave the limitations of the Enlightenment for the mystical and mythic realm, in the spirit of C.S. Lewis and J.R.R. Tolkien, and create a story that will unearth the buried monsters of the empires that have connected the entire world in electric light.

Each Act will be released as a single volume, with accompanying original illustrations. The complete poem will then be released in a lavish omnibus edition boasting 500 stanzas and 125 full-page illustrations.

JOIN US AT DRAGONCOMMONROOM.COM

WRITING
CHRISTIAN
POETRY

Writing Christian Poetry

A DRAGON COMMON ROOM COLLECTION

EVITA PILAR DUFFY-ALFONSO   LINDSEY ESSELMAN
MATTHEW HECK   CONRAD MOJICA   ANA RATH
JACQUES REYNOIR   AN ANONYMOUS SCHOLAR

EDITED BY
RACHEL FULTON BROWN

979-8-218-25360-8 *Print*
979-8-218-25361-5 *Ebook*

www.dragoncommonroom.com

Then the Lord answered Job out of a whirlwind, and said:
"Who is this that wrappeth up sentences in unskilful words?
Gird up thy loins like a man: I will ask thee, and answer thou me.
Where was thou when I laid the foundations of the earth? Tell me
*   if thou hast understanding.*
Who hath laid the measures thereof, if thou knowest or who hath
*   stretched the line upon it?*
Upon what are its bases grounded? Or who laid the cornerstone
*   thereof,*
when the morning stars praised me together, and all the sons of
*   God made a joyful melody?"*

—Job 38:1-7

Contents

Introduction

RACHEL FULTON BROWN

I have no business writing poetry. I have no formal training in writing poetry; I have never taken a course in writing poetry; the only poems I have published have been long-form narratives that I wrote with a group of amateurs whom I assembled on the social media platform Telegram, and occasional verses that I have posted on my blog *Fencing Bear at Prayer*. And yet, in Autumn 2021, I offered a course at the University of Chicago on "Writing Christian Poetry," for which ten students enrolled.[1]

The course was cross-listed in History, Religious Studies, Medieval Studies, and the History of Christianity. We had no textbook on writing poetry, although we did have a handbook on the arts of the trivium which included sections on meter and rhyme (John Martineau), and we had readings in the history of European Latin literature (Ernst Robert Curtius), the laughter at the heart of Christian literature (Anthony Esolen), Christian theology and the poetic imagination (Malcolm Guite), and the spiritual history of English literature (Andrew Thornton-Norris).[2]

There was one assignment for the quarter, with no exceptions: write 50 stanzas of eight lines each in iambic pentameter (400 lines total) on a Christian theme of your choice. All ten students rose to the challenge; seven of their poems are published here.

I have taught at the University of Chicago for nearly thirty years. I have regularly included creative options in my assignments for final papers, for which students have frequently written poetry, including poems in Old English, Dwarvish, Elvish, Black Speech, and Portuguese for my course on "Tolkien: Medieval and Modern," and praises of Our Lady (in English and Latin) for my course on "Mary and Mariology," but this is the first course I have taught for which writing poetry, more particularly writing *Christian* poetry was a requirement. It was important for my pedagogical purposes that students were willing to do both, not because the course was intended as an exercise in conversion (although some students came to the course hoping for the context in which to explore such an experience), but because I wanted the students to learn something about the way in which Christianity depends on poetry for the expression of truth, as well as the practice of goodness and the experience of beauty.

Once upon a time, Christian education included training in meter and rhyme, particularly in Latin, because once upon a time, the arts of language were seen as bound up with the purpose of human existence: contemplating, serving, and praising God. As poet, philologist, and master story-teller J.R.R. Tolkien put it in "Mythopoeia," the poem he wrote to convince C. S. Lewis of the worth—and truth—of myths, most particularly Christian "myths":

> Blessed are the legend-makers with their rhyme
> of things not found within recorded time.[3]

Poetry is the art of putting language to music, of fitting words to the heartbeat of a meter. For Christians, this means participating in the work of the Creator—as Tolkien put it, in sub-creation—through imitation of God's great Artifact, Creation, made, as the Scriptures tell it, through the Word (John 1:1-3) according to number, weight, and measure (Wisdom 11:21). Modern secular poets have for the most part abandoned meter to work solely with words laid out in patterns on the page; read aloud, their poems are difficult to distinguish from prose. Conversely, medieval Christians had no word for what we call poetry or verse, writing even their prose in rhyme. What we call "poetry," they understood as "making" (*poiesis*) in all its rhetorical forms.[4]

What, then, is Christian poetry? We may think first of Dante Alighieri (d. 1321), writing rhyming, metrical verse in the vernacular at a time when Latin was considered the proper language for theology, but in English, Christian poetry begins somewhat earlier, back in the seventh century with the cowherd Caedmon, who was inspired to write verses on the stories of the Creation, the Fall, and Redemption—allegedly without any training in either theology or Latin verse. "Now," Caedmon sang at the behest of a certain someone who came to him in a dream,

...let us praise the Creator, Guardian
of the heavenly kingdom, his power and purpose,
his mind and might, his wondrous works.
He shaped each miraculous beginning,
each living creature, each earthly kind.
He first made for the children of men
Heaven as roof. Then our holy Shaper
crafted middle-earth, a home for mankind:

our God and Guardian watching over us—
eternal, almighty—our Lord and King.[5]

According to Bede, the venerable eighth-century historian of the Anglo-Saxon church, Caedmon's poems covered the whole narrative of the Scriptures from Genesis to Revelation, including the departure of Israel from Egypt, the incarnation, passion, resurrection, and ascension into Heaven of the Lord, the coming of the Holy Spirit and the teaching of the Apostles, as well as the "terrors of future judgement, the horrors of the pains of hell, and the joys of the heavenly kingdom."[6] For Caedmon, as for late antique Christian poets like Juvencus, Sedulius, Arator, and Avitus (not, to be sure, household names at present), poetry was primarily a form of narrative, a way of making the ancient stories of the Bible entertaining and accessible to new audiences, particularly when accompanied, as the ancient minstrels like King David sang them, on a harp.[7]

Much as today we would look to film makers to bring the biblical stories to life, in antiquity and throughout the Middle Ages, it was poets recasting the Bible in alliterative verse (Old England, Old Saxon) and hexameters (Latin) who appealed to popular audiences of courtiers, schoolchildren, and cowherds. By the time Dante was writing in the Florentine vernacular and Chaucer (d. 1400) was taking up his pen in Middle English, Christian writers had been telling stories for centuries in verse. Think *Star Wars* with John Williams's magnificent score—stories set to the music of rythmical language.[8] Many of these verses were lost with the advent of the printing press and, ironically, the shift to vernacular translations of the Scriptures (in prose), but the effect of centuries of Latin education persisted in the great rhythm of iambic pentameter: da-*dum* da-*dum* da-*dum* da-*dum* da-*dum*. If even today Shakespeare is revered for the beauty of his monologues or Milton is remembered for his epic portrayal of Satan, it is, arguably, the effect of their iambic pentameters as much as their words.

Language set to meter *means more* than prose; it has a structure and beauty that participates both in number and word. It is more than choice of vocabulary or clever figures of speech that gives metrical poetry its power; it is the very architecture of the cosmos, the music of the spheres, the grounding of language in both sound and sense. "The heavens are telling the glory of God," the psalmist sang. "And the firmament declareth the works of His hands." "Caeli enárrant glóriam Dei, et ópera mánuum ejus annúntiat firmaméntum," medieval Christians sang every morning. "Day unto day uttereth speech: and night unto night showeth knowledge" (Psalm 18, second psalm at Matins for the Little Office of the Virgin).[9] Christianity as understood throughout the Middle Ages was first and foremost a religion of praise of the Creator—as Caedmon put it, the "holy Shaper"—structured on the daily recitation of the psalms. Both clergy and laity recited them in Latin; children learned to read by reading the psalms. Accordingly, for one of the exercises in my course, I had the students participate in this tradition by rewriting a psalm in a meter of their choice—at which, through having to paraphrase the sense, they discovered the beauty of not only the words, but also the meter and sound.

Other exercises for the course included reading a favorite poem out loud to the class; writing twenty lines of iambic pentameter in heroic couplets (rhyming pairs) about a feast day of one's choice; choosing a model story (or parable) on which to structure a narrative; collecting materials on which to model characters, settings, and plot; thinking about rhetorical genre and style; writing a "Pixar-style" pitch for one's story; and outlining the plot for the poem stanza by stanza. We practiced elocution with McGuffy's Sixth Eclectic Reader and scansion by editing each other's lines. We talked about the way poems depend on breath and timing, phonemes and lexicon. Students critiqued each other's plots and characters, and we talked about symbolism and Augustinian *sermo humilis*. By the time we reached Gerard Manley Hopkins in our example readings, the students could hear Hopkins's "sprung rhythm" and appreciate the power of his alliterations. They could hear his banging on the anvil of his verse, forging his imagination (as Anthony Esolen, one of our critical guides, put it) in the "bonfire" of the mystery of the Incarnation.[10] And they could appreciate their own longing (as Tolkien put it) to "make still by the law in which we're made," hammering out the firmament as a tent "myth-woven and elf-patterned," and covered in jewels.

Will our verses encourage others to attempt the joys of the Word's poetic forge? It may seem extreme to say as much, but without poetry, Christianity dies. Not because it becomes less true, beautiful, or good, but because it ceases to live in our minds, imagination, and hearts. We become "scientific" and cold, the stars mere rocks, the heavens no longer a jewelled tent, but only a void. As Tolkien told Jack Lewis (in, we may note, iambic pentameter):

> He sees no stars who does not see them first
> of living silver made that sudden burst
> to flame like flowers beneath an ancient song,
> whose very echo after-music long

has since pursued. There is no firmament,
only a void, unless a jewelled tent
myth-woven and elf-patterned; and no earth,
unless the mother's womb whence all have birth.[11]

Both Tolkien and Lewis were enchanted with the ancient apperception of the music of the spheres—that celestial harmony created by the movement of the planets against the resounding tenor of the sphere of the fixed stars. This is the mathematical reality in which poetry moves: the measured beat of our breathing—in and out, in and out—against the movement of our language through time.

As Augustine put it in his meditation on music, it is this movement through time that our souls experience as ordered delight, wherein terrestrial things are subject to celestial, "and their time circuits join together in harmonious succession for a poem of the universe."[12] Creation itself is a poem, in which we participate by singing praises to God as Creator and Lord. In Malcolm Guite's words: "To hear snatches from the huge unknowable symphony of experience, to catch them and transpose them to a key that resonates with our understanding, so that at some point they harmonise with that unheard melody from heaven we are always trying to hear—that is the purpose of poetry."[13] To write Christian poetry in iambic pentameter is to recover the mystery at the heart of the Incarnation: the Word's entry into Creation; the Artist's entry into his Artifact, the Author's entry into his Story. Other meters may suit, to be sure, but iambic pentameter reminds us of who we are as creatures made in time, living insofar as our hearts beat to the rhythm of the stars.

Even more to the point, it matters that we *tell stories* in verse, not just seek to capture moods. The Gospels of Our Lord Jesus Christ are "good stories" (*godspell*)—good stories, moreover, that we, as Christians, believe are not just historically, but also allegorically, tropologically, and anagogically true. Ancient and medieval commentators talked about the "four senses" of Scripture according to which its stories might be read; now, for the most part, scholars of the Old Testament and New Testament acknowledge only the one (historical), arguably, again, because they no longer are able to read the Scriptures *as poetry*, carrying multiple layers of meaning, including the mystical or figural as well as the literal (economic, social, or political). As medieval Christians like Dante understood, Christianity depends upon the reading of the New Testament through the figures and tropes of the Old. Christ appears in the Old Testament in prophecies (figure or types), but in the New Testament in truth, historically fulfilling the prophecies veiled in the stories of the Old.

Poetry, like the Scriptures read Christologically, works on multiple levels, drawing correspondences between images that point to a higher or trascendent significance in such ordinary creatures as pigeons and bread. Tolkien talked about this sense of layered significance as characteristic of "fairy-stories," which he defined in turn as a genre of Gospel: "The Gospels," as he put it, "contain a fairy-story, or a story of a larger kind which embraces all the essence of fairy-stories." Like fairy-stories, the Gospels contain "marvels—peculiarly artistic, beautiful and moving: 'mythical' in their perfect, self-contained significance," among which "is the greatest and most complete conceivable eucatastrophe"—the Birth of Christ. As the most perfect fairy-story, the Gospel begins and ends as all true fairy-stories must—in joy—and for this reason, Tolkien insisted: "There is no tale ever told that men would rather find was true, and none which so many sceptical men have accepted as true on its own merits. For the Art of it has the supremely convincing tone of Primary Art, that is, of Creation. To reject it leads either to sadness or to wrath."[14]

Professor Esolen (also a poet) writes of the laughter embedded in the Christian reading of such Old Testament stories as the sacrifice of Isaac—the son of Abraham who was not sacrificed, but spared. God spared the son of Abraham, but as Christ, the Son of God, he did not spare himself, but carried the wood as, in the words of the Anglo-Saxon author of *Genesis A* (was it Caedmon?), "*wudu baer sunu.*" Grammatically, the phrase could be read either: "The son bore the wood," or (because in Old English *wudu* and *sunu* have identical forms in both the nominative and accusative cases) "The wood bore the Son." Esolen comments:

> Without dropping any other hint, the poet recalls to his audience a new field of significance, one unknown to Abraham and Isaac. The lad—from whom we hear not one word of protest against his father—foreshadows Christ, who carried the wood up another hill for a sacrifice, his own. Christ was Isaac, was the ram; Christ bore the wood to the altar, and *the wood bore him*. God spared the son of Abraham, but did not spare himself, so great was his love for the world.[15]

This is the understanding that telling the stories of the Scriptures in poetry unlocks: the vision of the world not just as a Creature, but as a Creature shot through with correspondences, echoes and reverberations of its making in time, and of God's love for his creatures and continuing care for them: "*wudu baer sunu.*" Poetry trains the eye and the ear, the mind and the imagination to catch glimpses of these shimmering traces of glory, ever-present but ignored when we read the world only for its material, literal meaning. Again, in Professor Esolen's words:

> To believe in a world governed by the all-wise and loving Father, who demands justice but whose very act of creation was a condescension, an act of mercy, is to know that divine providence is endlessly rich, embodied in the exploding galaxy and in the grain of sand on the shore. It is a world brimming with consequence: allusions shooting like weeds, wonderful and lush; paradoxes hidden like thrush's eggs in the tree-crotched nest; etymological parallels winking one to the other like the glaze of dewdrops on the first day. And as long as there are creatures like us, once naked in the garden, wise and innocent—now wise in our own minds, therefore foolish and half-blind and huddled up in disguises—the play of irony will thrive. We now experience irony mainly as that cold splash that wakes us, when we thought we knew what we did not; a child would experience it rather as that warm and sweet moment of wonder, when something whose meaning he did not know suddenly assumes its surprising and self-displaying place in the garden of knowledge and love and time, the created garden of God.[16]

Writing Christian poetry, even more so than reading Christian poetry, enables us to participate in this joyous wonder, to become childlike indeed in the play of sounds and sense, even as we confront the sorrows of our sins and our failure to rejoice always in the Lord. This is why poetry is not just a frivolous ornament, but rather *necessary* to Christian education: it is the discipline by which we discover both sorrow for our falling away from God and joy at his ever-present love. Esolen identifies this experience as irony; Tolkien called it eucatastrophe, that moment in a story when there is a turn, a catch of the breath, and a brimming of tears, as the veil of sorrow is pulled back and the joy hidden within revealed. It comes in *The Lord of the Rings* on the Field of Cormallen when Sam, having longed to hear the tale of his and Frodo's adventures told "as in the great tales," has all his dreams come true when the minstrel steps forth to sing "of Frodo of the Nine Fingers and the Ring of Doom,"at which point—as Tolkien puts it in "On Fairy-Stories"—there is "a piercing glimpse of joy, and heart's desire, that for a moment passes outside the frame, rends indeed the very web of story, and lets a gleam come through."[17] Again, as the narrator put it in *The Lord of the Rings*:

> And all the host laughed and wept, and in the midst of their merriment and tears the clear voice of the minstrel rose like silver and gold, and all men were hushed. And he sang to them, now in the elven-tongue, now in the speech of the West, until their hearts, wounded with sweet words, overflowed, and their joy was like swords, and they passed in thought out to regions where pain and delight flow together and tears are the very wine of blessedness.[18]

There is a persistent complaint among Christian parents about the poverty of modern story-telling, whether for adults or children. And there have been regular calls for more stories on the model of Tolkien and Lewis, but rarely is it acknowledged that what we are missing is not just stories, but narrative verse. Sam burst into tears as the minstrel stepped up *to sing* , much as Caedmon took up the harp and sang stories of the shaping of middle-earth, its sorrows and joys. Something is missing in our contemporary world, and it is not just stories, but stories in meter and rhyme. As Thornton-Norris observes in his account of our cultural and moral decay: "Prose is an art of literacy, and thus modern; but poetry is eternal, the cleansing of the tools of thought, their purification. That is why poetry is the fundamental literary art, the most spiritual, and the closest to music and to prayer."[19] Just as music expresses realities (mathematical, harmonious, celestial) that cannot be put into words, there are mysteries (symbolic, incarnational, transcendent) which cannot be paraphrased in prose.

With the loss of metrical narrative comes the loss of joy in modern story-telling because with the loss of meter comes the loss of the tension beteen reason and imagination on which the irony of Christianity depends. Witness the interminable printed and online debates about theology: there is little joy in such battles, because (as I read them) they are conducted not as experiments in wonder, but as exercises of domination and control. Poetry does not work the same way dialectic does. Dialectic, as Martianus Capella famously depicted her in his great pedagogical prosimetrum on the seven liberal arts, seeks to draw in opponents with her formulae (patterns or premises) so as to capture them with the serpent of her syllogisms. By contrast, Rhetoric seeks to capture the attention with beauty, rouse the emotions, and entertain, so as to move her audience to action, while Grammar concerns herself with proper pronunciation and the precision of names. Together, Grammar and Rhetoric produce speech that both inspires and moves, working at once on the imagination (adjectives and figures of speech) and on reason (naming), describing the world in ways that motivate us to make choices about how to behave. Dialectic convinces by leaving her opponents no logical way out; Grammar and Rhetoric persuade by moving their audiences to sorrow and joy.[20]

Here, then, is the true irony: without poetry, without the

work of the imagination on number and word, we lose access not only to beauty, but also to goodness and truth. Far from being "compound of lies" (as Lewis worried), the work of our imagintion is bound up with our perception and experience of Wisdom.[21] Without the images, associations, patterns, and intuitions of imagination, our reasoning about God and his Creation is incapable of perceiving truth. It becomes sterile and, ironically, unpersuasive, no matter how perfect its syllogisms and logical traps. The debate between the proponents of the three language arts goes back to the Middle Ages, but its effects are felt to this day: Dialectic may have "won" the "scientific" ground, but without Grammar and Rhetoric—without the arts of sounds, naming, and figures of speech—she is not wise, merely an unpersuasive bully who sees only "progressive apes, erect and sapient," and nothing of "the image blurred of distant king" in whose likeness those "progressive apes" were made.[22]

To be sure, that image and likeness includes reason, but it also includes the capacity to perceive symbolism—and enjoy play.

Glory be to God for dappled things—
For skies of couple-color as a brinded cow.[23]

We lose our humanity when we lose our capacity to participate in the joy of poetry, its allusions and assonances, echoes and counterpoint, ambiguities and ambivalence, sudden shocks and reversals, its irony and paradox. We lose our souls when we lose our desire to sing in praise of our Creator who "fathers-forth" in beauty in "all things counter, original, spare, strange."[24] Tolkien spoke of the magic of the adjective in activating the imagination —of the "green great dragon" whom he longed for in crafting his stories.[25] "The incarnate mind, the tongue, and the tale are in our world coeval."[26] To understand ourselves as made through the Word made flesh is to particpate in the joy of our own incarnation in the image and likeness of the Artist who made us. To celebrate our making in words crafted according to the rules of grammar and meter is to sing with the creatures made according to measure, weight, and number, disciplined by the rule in which they were made to resonate with the song of Creation. As the Lord told Job: on the day of creation, the morning stars praised him and all the sons of God—the angels—sang for joy (Job 38:7).

Writing Christian poetry is, properly speaking, an exercise (a practice, a discipline, an art) in recovering the joy at being creatures of a loving and beautiful Creator. Much as creation itself, it works on multiple levels—physical and mental, sensory and intellectual, verbal and mathematical—to participate in the experience of the morning stars on the first day, praising God in jubilant melody. That we have lost this discipline or reduced it (as Professor Esolen laments) to child's play ("childen clapping their hands in a kindergarten jingle") and (as Tolkien sorrowed) consigned it to the lumber room with the fairy-stories and mythologies we are too "grown up" to believe, is not only a witness to our sophistication as Enlightened *philosophes*; it is also the cause of our descent into madness, the collapse of our culture, and the death of our ability to reason.[27] Do you doubt me? When was the last time you looked up to the stars and saw the glory of God spangled across the heavens as on the first day when the angels sang? When was the last time you saw the reality of the firmament as a jewelled tent and wondered at the mystery of the Artist's entry into his Creation through the veil of the Virgin's womb?

Do you want to save our culture? Ask yourselves rather: do you want to practice our proper cult—praising and giving thanks to our Maker and God? Do you want to look up into the heavens and hear the music of the spheres and shout with joy at the mystery of being incarnate minds made in the image and likeness of their Maker? Do you want to rejoice at the birth of God in time to remake his creatures through love? There is an easy solution: Learn to beat out the meter in which our greatest poems in English were written. Learn to hear the sounds of the words in which we tell our stories of the Creation, Fall, and Redemption. Learn to see the patterns and figures through which God communicates to his creatures, the numbers by which he crafted the cosmos and the symbols through which they are named. Learn to listen for melodies in phonemes and rhythms in stress; learn to name things precisely and pronounce their names. Learn to write stories true to the resonances and allusions of myth; learn to write stories in which reality breaks through and in which "Legend and History have met and fused."[28] Learn to see the stars in a single syllable and God's truth, goodness, and beauty in a grain of sand.

Learn to scan.

THE STUDENTS' POEMS

Each of the following poems was written in response to the same prompt: "Write a poem of 50 stanzas of 8 lines each (400 lines total) on a Christian theme of your choice." Everything else was up to the students: topic, mood, references, genre. Some students wrote poems based on their own experiences; others wrote stories drawing on historical models or themes. Some invented realistic scenarios; others drew on dreams and fantasies. There was no requirement for the poems to take any particular theological position other than incarnational, nor were the students expected themselves to be Christians (although most were). The challenge was to write in meter on a Christian theme—historical, allegorical, moral, or anagogical, as the students chose. It is all the more remarkable how varied their poems are, given how closely they worked over the course of the quarter on references and meter, almost as if writing about the whole of history, the beauty of Creation, and the longing for virtue were liberating, rather than constrained. It is also remarkable how many of their poems deal with sorrow and death.

It is best, I think, to let the poems speak for themselves, although I will say they all make me cry, albeit in a good way, tears of joy as the veil is pulled back, and a gleam beyond the web of story is revealed. Whether in Somebody's quest for the reality of devotion to "made-up" saints like Nobody or Expedite, or in the Birdkeeper's son's allegorical wrestling with the real-life death of his father, we see the longing for assurance that the story is true, while with the dream-vision of the soldier, saying his rosary with his legs blown off, or with the king who has his wife executed on the basis of a rumor, we explore the poignancy of choice. The death of a beloved husband, the escape of a mother and her children from the leftist Republicans of Spain, a debate between brothers over the life choices they made—the poems resist paraphrase, much as (according to Bede) Caedmon's verses resisted translation. Like all good stories, much of their poignancy lies in the telling, made all the more so by the constraints of the meter to find just the right word. If nothing else, this was the most important lesson I hoped the students would take from the course: that in poetry, as in world-building, every word counts.

As do the silences. I may have no business writing poetry in praise of Our Lord Jesus Christ, but then neither did the psalmist —or the saints. As St. Expedite learns in his poetic quest:

"Nobody has seen God!" (John 1:18) And yet, as Ronald assured his friend Jack, in Paradise:

> ... poets shall have flames upon their heads,
> and harps whereon their faultless fingers fall:
> there each shall choose for ever from the All.[29]

Of Expedite, Procrastinators' Saint

SOMEBODY, A SCHOLAR

I

Before the story starts, I ought to pray:
please grant your intercession, Expedite!
So that I might begin, without delay,
the legendary tale of your Good Fight.
Come help me, not tomorrow but today,
to wake my soul and type the story right.
Hence, smash the dullness devil, do it swith,
and hear, at once, this true and holy myth.

Three-hundred three AD, Malatya region:
the Roman troops are stationed on alert.
Though Persians ran with fear from "Thunder Legion,"
the *Fulminata* leader is inert
by news about the Jesus Christ Religion.
His heart is moved. He asks: "Should I convert?"

A creepy crow cries: "Cras!" cries: "Cras!" cries: "Cras!"
Cruel creature, creaky, cranky, crafty, crass!

The Roman chief decides: "It is tomorrow!"
But then, tomorrow came and nothing changed.
The lagger devil came, the evil sparrow,
again, it shouted "Cras!" in screech deranged.
The man obeyed with laziness and sorrow,
yet feeling faint, from earthly state estranged.
"Enough!", he said at last, "Christ *is* the Way!"
He crushed the sinful bird and cried: "Today!"

The bloody Diocletian Persecution,
determined to contain the Christian spread,
condemned the Roman chief to execution:
his faith, though fresh, did make them cut his head.
But God in heaven gave him absolution
and raised his happy soul from body dead.
Now, dwelling where there holds no ill or taint,
is Expedite! Procrastinators' saint!

Around the world, across the land and ocean,
wherever reaches Christian faith profession,
his fame provokes a fervent firm devotion.
Somewhere he's praised with crowded large procession;
elsewhere, a simple pious kneeling motion:
each one has his (or her) distinct expression.
His cult keeps spreading out as time goes by.
Miraculous accounts still multiply.

Above this altar stands a statuette

of *Expeditus*, wearing cape and sandals,
subduing "*cras*" in raven silhouette.
And, right in front, a heap of flaming candles.
The faithful come in haste, afraid, upset:
for urgent matters are the ones he handles.
If just and due, this saint does any task,
provided that—with hope and faith—you ask.

This one forgot to study for the term:
he prays because he needs a rapid fix.
That one was just laid off by bankrupt firm:
"He'll find me gainful work soon"—she predicts.
And that has throbbing pains that make him squirm:
tried lotions, pills, vaccines. He's out of tricks.
The sculpted martyr deals with any ail,
no matter timing, worthiness, or scale.

These people need results at lofty speed.
Knelt down, they keep hands joined and foreheads bowed.
The statuette pays heed to every plead:
it likes to be esteemed by pious crowd.
The saint it represents shall help concede.
When all is solved, the sculpture feels quite proud.
"How great am I?" it thinks, "was that not stunning?"
It lauds itself for alien skill and cunning.

Elsewhere, in narrow stuffy murky room,
with walls wrapped up in books, scant space between,
a skeptic academic drowned in gloom,
distinguished scholar (bearing double chin),
low-whispers: "Now the saint will meet his doom,"

and then he smiles with cynic evil grin.
He gets a heavy book from far-off shelf,
then, when he reads it, he delights himself.

"This legend has no true historic ground!
Saint Expedite is but a childish lie!"
Murmuring low, with most annoying sound,
the scholar says, while giving haughty sigh:
"I'll spread the shocking data that I found.
This cult is over now, that I decry."
He claims, the noted sage agnosticist:
"Alas, Saint Expedite does not exist!"

II

The scholar's findings scattered far and wide.
"This saint, so-called, is mythical: not real!
If Expedite has never lived nor died,
then why do still the foolish faithful kneel?"
Some scorn the saint with sneery comments snide,
but many carry on with love and zeal
the pleas to such an excellent ally,
insisting that the saint is not a lie.

Iconoclastic critics with no qualms
demand the tossing of the fake façade:
"Tear down the statues, with their martyr's palms,
of phony heathen idol, made-up god.
Their actual function is stockpiling alms
from folk naïve who cannot see the fraud!"
These vexing words end up instilling doubt

in honest hearts, no matter how devout.

In this church here the dreadful claims arrive,
although in whispers low and hard to hear.
One should not speak in church unless to shrive,
yet murmurs float across the nave unclear.
Ill gossiping in idle spirits thrive.
The statue hears the news and shakes with fear:
"Am I a mere sham idol carved of oak?
This whole darn time, was I some stupid joke?!"

"If I'm a sculpture of some cult profane,
if I'm no more than painted wood and grout,
then people pray to Expedite in vain,
for he can't hear the calls of his devout.
But how is this? Will anyone explain?
My existence should not be put in doubt!
This vital riddle I don't understand.
A meaningful response hence I demand."

The statuette decides on stepping down
from sacred altar, quitting holy state.
Behind it leaves its shining martyr's crown,
and then it walks across the temple gate,
in search for said sly scholar of renown
who tried with words to terminate its fate.
Now, where will this bizarre adventure lead?
Can troubled sculpted Expedite succeed?

The living sculpture left abrupt the church,
distressed by blunt apparent fall from grace.

And for a long while it conducted search
for academic's home, in hurried pace.
"With what design did you myself besmirch?"
it asked, just when it found the scholar's place.
Instead of answers, though, No One replied:
"Too late," Nobody said, "the scholar died."

When No One spoke, the fearful statue stalled.
Afraid, it asked in whisper: "Who are you?"
A voice replied: "Nobody I am called."
"Nobody's here?!", it yelled; "this can't be true."
The *Expeditus* sculpture was appalled.
It asked No One: "Am I nobody, too?"
Nobody said: "To be nobody's good;
if no one you could be, I'm sure you would.

"I am the Nemo from the Sacred Writ.
I lived through global flood plus grim disasters.
Nobody (yes, that's me) has God-like wit.
I am the only one who serves two masters.
Because I never sinned, I will admit:
I'd be among adulteress stone-casters.
I even blinded Cyclops from tale Greek.
No One is this strong, perfect and unique.

"Therefore, were you no one, you should rejoice!
Because that means you carry matchless might!"
Thus spoke No One in eerie, pitchless voice.
The statue heard it, quivering with fright.
And then Nobody said: "So, make your choice!
You want to be No One or Expedite?"

The sculpture liked Nobody's words' allure,
but there was something there somewhat obscure...

And then, Nobody laughed and said: "You see?
All told, this scholar was, at most, a pawn.
He taught and wrote, while showing vain degree,
but, in the end, it's over. Now he's gone.
Nobody can escape mortality.
Exclusively Nobody will live on."
With this, the statue said at last: "It's done.
I want to have the power of No One."

III

Through path irregular and serpentine,
No One and statuette began to climb.
The upward path soon led them to a shrine,
abandoned building of a distant time,
atop a hill, of stone, in Goth design,
impassive ruins veiled by dust and grime.
Nobody said: "I come up here a lot.
There's nothing here. That's why I like this spot."

The statue goes inside the ruin bleak.
And there, an awful sighting makes it cower:
a human-bodied huge dog-headed freak.
The sculpture cries out: "Please, don't me devour!"
The cynocephalus replies: "What do you seek?"
The statue says: "I want Nobody's power."
"What do you mean?! Is this some kind of jest?!
Fear me, Christopher, patron saint of quest."

Behind Christopher, two more figures stand.
"I'm Philomena, patron saint of youth,"
says gracious girl with arrows on her hand.
"And I am Barbara, murdered for the Truth
for shunning vile apostasy demand.
We're saints. We all defeated Belzebuth.
Enormous crowds our images revere.
So, say again, my friend. Why are you here?"

The sculpture answered solemnly, knee-bending:
"I want to have far-reaching global heft,
and, most of all, I want a life unending.
When I was lost, of holiness bereft,
I had the fortune of No One befriending..."
It stopped and looked around. No One had left.
"No One was here!", it says, "did you not see?
Nobody was just here! Was it just me?!"

Christopher shouts: "You're mad! We are somebody!"
The statue cries: "I know! So is Nobody!"
"You mean Nobody's just like anybody?"
"In fact, Nobody outranks everybody."
"You think a god Nobody does embody?
For sure, Nobody's not The Holy Body!"
They halt their chat. Someone came in the shrine.
It's Catherine, martyr saint Alexandrine!

Says Catherine: "Stop this farce. Do not be fools,
misusing time in chat superfluous!
While we chit-chat, No One us ridicules.
Nobody has confused us, treasonous,

transformed us into ex-saints, hopeless ghouls,
and on our altars stands, replacing us.
We have to kick Nobody out, for starters.
And then, return, as statues of great martyrs."

Thus spoke Saint Catherine, with her breaking wheel.
And all the others listened with dismay.
Christopher asked her: "Wait. Am I not real?"
And Catherine answered: "That I did not say.
We all are made of wood or stone or steel.
Though physical, Divine Grace we convey.
Material, by the spirit vivified,
we're similar to Jesus crucified.

"It's worth remembering a basic rule:
the one who honors icons made of matter,
to image lights a blaze or gives oscule,
that faithful one is not iconolater.
That one is a devout iconodule.
Thus with us saints. Thus with Beata Mater."
Christopher answered: "Yes. This does make sense.
I am with you. Let Holy Quest commence!"

Then Barbara spoke, while holding golden chalice:
"I'm with you, Catherine and Christopher, wholly.
We shall engage against Nobody's malice.
How come No One is dwelling in House Holy,
as if the church could be Nobody's palace?
We ought to put an end to this sick folie.
So, let's design, right now, attack plan thorough."
Saint Catherine asks: "What day is it tomorrow?"

Saint Barbara says: "Tomorrow's Hallowmas."
"Indeed", says Catherine, "What a fitting day!
Let's strike No One before the All-Saints mass.
You with me? We must throw No One away!"
(A raven, ravenous, cruel crow, cries "CRAS!")
Thinks Expedite: "I'm going to here stay."
"The Saints are needed for All Hallows feast,"
states Catherine. "We'll be there, us five, at least."

IV

Now, here, this church is grimmer than a grave
dug deep. Replete with cumbersome pitch-black
thick silent emptiness. Inside the nave
there are no images, and altars lack
their lights and relics. You can't your soul lave
for there's no holy water. What a sack!
No frankincense ascends and bells don't ring:
Nobody occupies just everything.

Before side-altar stands a devotee,
with eyes distressed but an expression candid.
The simpleton recites: "I pray to Thee,"
despondently, with arms crosswise expanded.
Before a niche with Null, he bends the knee.
But soon he'll go back home flat empty-handed.
Nobody will his pious prayers shun.
No One gives nothing to just everyone.

The same thing happens to so many pleas:
this crying woman, with despairing sob,

asks empty niche the cure for ill disease;
and this man supplicates to get a job;
and this asks: "Get the paperwork done, please!"
But there's no way to satisfy the mob:
pleads to Nobody never are conceded.
Today Saint Expedite is truly needed.

Saint Catherine cries that there's no time to wait:
"We must our altars now again reclaim,
and stop all those who do them desecrate."
Christopher heeds. The others do the same,
except for Expedite, who seems distrait.
He merely mumbles: "That is not my aim.
I have not traveled here in search of thrills.
I only want to have Nobody's skills."

These words left Catherine very much annoyed:
"You fool don't know? The crowd continues praying.
Poor things, they don't know that they were decoyed.
They keep intentions on the altar laying,
but rather than with saints they plead with Void.
They need us back. Let's go! We are not staying.
Nobody must be crushed! Please join us! Come!"
"In light of that", the statue mutters, "hmmm...

"In light of that... I'll give to this some thought."
(The crafty creaky crow "Tomorrow!" cries.)
"You're right. It's bad that people pray to Naught,
instead of Holy God up in the Skies.
But all this stir and hustle we need not.
You go ahead," says Expedite unwise;

"Godspeed, my holy friends! I'll meet you later!"
To this, Christopher answers: "You're a traitor."

Saint Catherine questions Expedite: "You sure?"
Nonchalant Expedite replies: "I'm so.
It looks to me decision premature
to strike already such unthreatening foe.
Should we not stay here, in the shrine, secure?"
(Foul fowl flies forth criss-cross cries, "CRAS!" crass crow.)
"All right", says Catherine, "we'll leave you alone.
Goodbye, Saint Expedite. You're on your own."

October thirty-one, before sunset.
The band of sculpted martyrs resolute
is ready to Nobody's church beset.
"*Deus vult!*" shouts Catherine. Barbara follows suit.
And Saint Christopher likewise cries with threat.
Saint Philomena also yells a hoot.
They fiercely scream while crossing the narthex:
"Begone who iconoduly rejects!"

Soon after they inside the temple stepped,
they realized they could not No One find.
They searched the nave, the apse, and the transept,
and each side-altar through the aisles aligned.
Some hours later, having all church swept,
the martyrs thought with woe: "We must be blind!"
"It's pointless," said Cristopher, "No One's here!"
"Exactly," Catherine claimed, "that's plainly clear."

Saint Catherine looked around with grave concern:

"A thousand altars bare and niches hollow,
A somber scene of ruin, I discern.
In sacred space, Nobody should not wallow.
The cult of saints must urgently return.
More saints ought our good example follow.
But we cannot defeat No One. We're few.
How will we quickly get so large a crew?"

V

Christopher says: "The timing's way too tight.
We'd have to grow a thousand-fold in size
before the end of this All Saints' Eve night.
We cannot such large party mobilize,
regardless of how fast we expedite."
"Did you say Expedite?" Saint Catherine cries;
"That's it! Saint Expedite's great skill Divine!
We'll ask his help. Let's go! Back to the shrine!"

Inside the shrine, is Expedite distressed.
The sculpture struggles with an inner strife:
"I muted every prayerful request,
since I gave up my previous holy life.
My life's true meaning I therefore suppressed.
With selfish beings like me this world is rife.
I willingly did fall in No One's trap."
(Foul fowl flaps flapping floppily flip-flap!)

Saint Expedite addresses evil thrush:
"Today your idler goals you won't achieve!"
He stomps on demon bird with heavy *crush*!

"Right now! My time has come! I have to leave."
Saint Catherine barges in: "We're in a rush!
We need your urgent help this All Saints' Eve!
A thousand saints we need you to enlist!
'Gainst such an army No One won't subsist."

"I'll summon sculpted saints from everywhere,
and ask for help against these chances dire.
The God's elects will make No One despair.
No One will learn that Saints do not retire.
Confronted with Jehovah's just and fair,
I'm certain that Nobody will expire."
Thus spoke Saint Expedite with shining eyes,
and promptly started rounding up allies.

Saints Ursula, Chrysogonus, Tryphon,
the Forty Martyrs of Sebaste, Hyginus,
Marcellus, Eustace, Sennen and Abdon,
Faustinus and Jovita, Zephyrinus,
the Holy Machabees, Pantaleon,
Alexius, Prisca, Cletus, Marcellinus,
Sylvester, Valentine, and hundreds more,
adhered to Expeditus's call to war.

The holy host yells joyfully: *"Deus vult!"*
and bursts inside the church at potent rate.
They uninstall No One's ungodly cult,
begin to sacred spacc repopulate,
and finally, they revel and exult,
for God Nobody did annihilate.
Replacing now Nobody's barren spells

are vitrals, relics, hymns, incense, and bells.

And now the church is filled with golden light
and with Gregorian chants that never falter.
The faithful come inside to reunite
and sing together from the holy psalter.
Amazed with all this sight is Expedite.
Yet now it's time to climb back to his altar.
But when he starts to climb, he hears a voice.
A pitchless voice: "So did you make your choice?"

"No One? What an unpleasant *déjà vu!*",
says Expedite, while grasping firm his sword,
"Why are you still in here? You're way past due!"
No One replies: "You think you please the Lord?
Perhaps you have forgotten you're not true!
Misleading simple folk for cash reward."
And Expedite: "Stop this absurd truth-twist!
It's you, Nobody, that does not exist.

"Yes, I am mythical, but I'm no lie.
I bring forth Jesus Christ similitude.
Indeed, saints' lives of God do testify
and holy icons are of Grace imbued.
But what of you, No One? You God deny.
I'll end you now, for once! Don't me elude.
Why don't you go to hell, you wicked *demo?*
Hear, I command you: *VADE RETRO, NEMO!*"

When No One was at long last overturned,
the whole church celebrated Halloween;

the organ *tutti* played, and candles burned:
a setting wonderful, before unseen.
As time went by, No One no more returned.
And everyone went back to life-routine.
Today—I've been there—on that very site,
upon his altar stands Saint Expedite.

The King of Songs

MATTHEW HECK

I

We set our story in a dozen realms,
ruled jointly by one king sat at the helm.
Beneath, in fief, preside a dozen dukes:
themselves once kings, who were by God rebuked.
No treasure trove, nor knightly valor bold,
could halt the King nor victory withhold.
He spared the vanquished, though, to win allegiance,
for souls no better serve when ruled by grievance.

In lines of five, towards palace incomplete,
proceed those who had lost their royal seats
on horses proud in polished plate and mail
accompanied by counts in noble trail,
their garments bright and not once prior worn,
their arms displayed on silken banners borne.

Then followed carts of gifts with each parade
and filled the growing city's promenade.

Each man-at-arms then brandished metal spears.
All halted. Silence reigned and all could hear:
a man from Veisya introduced his call
to tell of those that our great king enthralled
and narrate this procession's benefits.
T'wards this, he used their art named "Rhetoric."
He bows then clears his throat before he starts.
Each realm and gift he lists, concise and smart:

"Rich Veisya of canals and wisdom old
was first: his future empire they foretold.
The Marquis grants a thousand red, clay jars
filled up with that pure honey sweet of ours.
Kalehn fell next, that house of equity,
where justice sprouts from its straight cedar trees,
they bring a thousand silver rings, at least,
with perfect pearls imported from the East.

"Dominion, next, he forged from fractured parts
for his young brother, dearest in his heart.
From countless cities called to meet his whim:
a hundred craftsman skilled with bronze and tin.
Now to Ancora, in the West, he moved
and through a contest the Great Chieftain proved.
Their men present two dozen thoroughbreds,
all charcoal studs, except their white-streaked heads.

"He sailed South now and won Verandia's crown

her king afraid to be, by death, cast down:
The Summer Duke bears gold and scarlet wines,
matured and aged from his exquisite vines.
Sengre's yoke, then, he trampled underfoot
and cast off cruel, degrading slavery's soot.
They give rare potions t'ease the sorrows of
our ceaseless waking, wounds, and forlorn love.

"Otraina's plateaued cities vast he saw,
whose engines could not spare them from his maw.
This tool they crafted and precisely tuned
predicts the union of the Sun and Moon.
The Eternal City, storied seat of gods,
with towers white, was last to feel his rod.
Three dozen bolts of woven gold they pay,
befitting him who rose above the fray.

"But swords are not sufficient to impose
that unity sworn in our solemn oaths.
Before him, each realm worshipped many gods,
but revelation struck like lashing rod:
God told our king that all things are His agents:
the 'gods' but messengers who serve as regents.
Each 'god' was charged, of old, to heed men's sighs,
yet worship false each sought to beautify."

The gifts now laid before their grateful king,
intent resided there in everything,
the lords knelt down to pledge him loyalty:
"In lieu of you, we take viceroyalty,
and pledge to heed your just and right decrees.

This we shall do until gripped by death's freeze."
A solemn nod confirmed his majesty,
before he spoke with regal clarity:

"Come, celebrate this joyous day with me!
Let this child's birthright be tranquility!
Let malice drown in that eternal sleep
induced by poisoned draught in chalice deep.
Resent not your late loss of liberty;
instead, rejoice at new security!
Now wash away cruel thoughts with endless drink,
and let us all in amity be linked."

II

The great bronze palace gates swung open wide,
revealing the paved courtyard there inside:
in form, a square with double colonnade,
its opulence left all who looked amazed.
Materials he had brought from far flung lands
and carved with delicate conceits by hand.
Desiring, though, the promised bacchanal,
they left, to eat, for the reception hall.

Though three lone men held back and there remained
and contemplated what submission gains.
Sengre's sly duke, the primate of the lot,
approached the lesser lords, their thoughts he sought:
"Such riches I have never seen, I swear..."
"Nor I," rejoined the one with southern air,
"when visiting th'Eternal City's wealthy.

Verandia sees it not in years of plenty..."

"What would you say," the Duke then whispered soft,
"if I could lay low he who is aloft?"
"What speak you of?" the Goldbend priest inquires:
"Do you now offer what we all desire?
Yet why should I trust one of your sly race?
All know you lie yet wear a pleading face!"
"Why lie?" Sengre asks, "hatred spurs us on.
We all do hope the King's last day soon dawns.

"Has he not placed a demon on the throne?
Withdrawn the gods from their eternal home?
High Heaven's King a tired servant made,
now acting as this nameless Father bade.
And you, O lord, of fruitful southern farms,
does not this state thy people's honor harm?
The proper order this low shepherd lord
usurped when your crowned king laid down his sword!"

"A murder wants more than a motive strong.
It needs a means and plans to hide the wrong,"
this said, the Southern count stood waiting, eager.
"My plan is at this moment plain and meagre—"
"That matters not: three minds can fast fill gaps."
"I plan to guide our despot to a trap
and there he'll tumble down without foreknowledge
or else, as heir, another's son acknowledge."

"A plot as one would find in child's tales, duke,"
began the Priest, "applied, though, they're no fluke.

If I'm to undertake this enterprise,
 don't leave me to particulars surmise."
"Rare prudence drips from each and every phrase,"
the Duke said: "Let me guide you through this maze.
For all are in one way susceptible
to thoughts completely unacceptable."

"The son's the key," the Duke began with speed:
"All fathers hope their sons shall them exceed.
With magic draughts, we'll lure his wife to sleep.
Then pull a servant from his household's heap
and drug him too and lay them both abed.
Him I'll alert with something slyly said;
he'll rush to make this cruel discovery,
and he—to all his fiefs—shall cuckold be."

"A tremor this would send to psyche's base..."
the Priest then mused: "Lay out the time and place!"
The Duke then glanced, ensuring they're alone:
"My gift was our narcotic stepping-stone:
the Queen's in feminine confinement kept,
so priestly bribes shall make a guard inept;
our southern lord shall then our servant snatch
and both, to sleep, shall quickly be dispatched."

"'Tis carefully and well contrived, think I—"
"Hold off, my southern friend," the Priest replied:
"In plots of treason in my Metropol,
great promises are made to pay each role—"
"Great sums of money I can pay you now,
or vast assurances, just tell me how.

Confine yourselves, though, not to present pay,"
the Duke exhorted in impassioned way:

"Just think: high offices shalt thou obtain
for thy king's fall brought dour and sundry rains,
yet restoration promises rewards...
What's more, grace surely falls on he, in hoards,
who, stalwart, piously defends his god
and leaves all false, impure apostates awed."
"To this ignoble treason we assent...
for this false lordling everyone resents."

III

The Queen was overtaken one week thence;
her labor, long awaited, then commenced.
The noble vassals gathered there to wait
for news of their new prince's fate.
The inner courtyard filled with huddled groups,
as not one man was permit in her coop.
As more arrived, each whispered of their shock:
Sengre's duke came before they'd yet heard talk.

"Hail, king! My lord, where go you on your way?"
"How now, my faithful vassal of Sengre?
To visit my new son, just born. What luck!"
"Of course! I say, you're always fortune struck.
But loyalty compels me to this ask,
for I thought you did not give eunuchs tasks,
and yet, to enter the Queens chambers, he
a doughy *castrati* must surely be?"

"This bodes not well, at least for honor's sake..."
began the King. "My faith in her does quake...
Yet... nay! Until indicted by clear facts,
my trust in her will not be found to lack!
A man, forbid, corrupts her safe retreat,
so there we go! And there the truth we'll meet!
If true... I fear I must resort to force..."
Replied the Duke: "That seems the proper course!"

Unto her quarters they, without delay,
the guards withdrew, aside, out of their way.
These chambers always bustled with her maids,
yet now stand empty: peaceful as a glade.
And there! Embracing like two peasant lovers,
reclined upon green grass beneath tree cover,
lay Queen and butler, out without a sound.
Awoke they then! As chaos rose all-round!

"You whore! You dare defile our marriage bed?"
the King accused. "You have not ceased to shed
the blood of birth before you lie in sin!
I wish 'twere not, but else could not have been...
I'd laugh it off if yestermorn I'd learned
that my son's birth would me have overturned!
To think you were the type for chastity...
No more! I see that all is vanity!"

Her wits, in part, recovered, she arose:
"Outrageous lies spread you, and unopposed!"
She cast her gaze around and to her right
and tumbled from her bed, such was her fright.

"This man is foreign to my loyal eyes!
To enter here... so closely supervised...
My prince, my lord, my love, I know not how!
A hunch would point to those who falsely bow!"

"Endeavor ye to cast such baseless blame
when you find your feet pressed up to the flame?"
The King now spit each word with frothy wrath:
"Would you dunk me into a shit-filled bath
to later say I smelled of roses fresh?
'Tis clear! This child and I share not same flesh!
What would you have me do? Deny my vision?
Yet still! 'Tis true! Confirmed by fickle reason!"

Once regal Queen the guards then bound in shame
and dragged out to the yard, her feet gone lame.
No warning had they of what's to come,
no time to raise a scaffold 'neath the sun.
Instead, a headsman's block upon the ground,
its wood was sure to make his "thwack" resound.
The Queen fell down, her eyes lit by a tear.
Yet after, none said she showed any fear...

"A pension he'll receive until the last
for such does equitable justice ask..."
This said the King unto himself, and then:
"Bring out that bastard! Cause of all this din?"
The midwife babbling with her newborn charge,
emerged: events to her remained at large.
"Oh such a healthy child I've never seen!
The only mark is, on his back, a bean!"

"Reason abandons me!" cried he; "Oh, how
the worldly throne is rendered barren now!
Iniquity, that foul disease, have I
invited in: deflowered by a lie!
Undone, my line of kings, before their hour...
A regal mother? None! Just stillborn sour...
For this small child is mine, to this I'll swear...
this mark my father bore and I still bear!"

IV

He buckled, falling with a horrid shriek.
He tumbled there, the mighty rendered meek.
His clothes he rent and let fall, baring skin,
no more the conqueror he had once been...
He passed a minute in unspoken thought,
then scrambled up and rushed off like a shot.
Through crowd perplexed and palace gate he fled,
towards Father's Temple, clear ahead.

Through golden doors and past the Temple's crewmen,
not heeding laws against a presence human.
Between the Seraph gold, he knelt and wept:
"You promised to protect my royal sept!
If fooled by lies, reveal them all to me,
and punish them for all eternity!
If I'm confounded by my foes, then smite!
If I'm deceived by demons foul, then fight!"

"God helps not men who violate His Law,"
said voice quite feminine. He spun in awe.

She was more terrible, to his dismay,
than any army he'd seen in array.
"How got you here?" Pressed he, "'tis restricted!"
"Forbid to man, yet now by thee afflicted!"
rejoined the spirit. "God sent me,
since thou would subjugate the Law to thee."

"Is God so fickle to abandon me,
enactor of His will divine?" said he:
"I've offered choicest meats to His bright flames,
proclaimed across the world His holy name,
conformed to countless, all of His decrees.
What's more, I purged false heresy's disease!
As he each order gave, I saw no flaw,
but now complete, His favor He withdraws!"

"Thine arrogance pollutes this sanctum pure!"
said she in righteous fury: "Be demure!
To worship, sacrifice is but the least;
to suffer rules does not make thee a priest;
to order Man, for peace, God thee installed;
to sit in prudent judgement, thou wert called,
but when thy loyal wife lay there accused,
in wrath, thou killed her, trial, fair, refused."

"Oh, Everlasting Father, name your terms,
and I shall meet them: I'm Your servile worm!
As punishment severe may satisfy
Justice divine; 'tis sin to You defy!"
With thund'rous voice and echo from the deep:
"Thine foul transgressions doth make me to weep.

For grievous murder there be but one price:
to feel the pain of death, not once, but thrice.

"Choose wisely of my proffered options three;
with one fulfilled, your grace restored shall be.
A famine deadly shall befall your vale
and sweep away joy, leaving only wails,
or else a plague upon your capital:
The mirror of its royal, fallible,
and yet, your ultimate choice still remains:
to feel and risk death's permanent, dark pain."

"What choices… famine, plague, or death's embrace…
Dead bodies would her memory debase…
Should peasants whither due to my quick ire?
Should burghers suffer under fever's fire?
Or should I bear the judge's penalty?
My suffering could be her elegy…
Her pain I'll bear, for reason this expects:
who gives offense shall not the cost neglect."

"The proper choice," the LORD proclaimed to him:
"Now heed my words and know that they're my whim:
I charge thee now and on until they end
to each dispute, through prudent judgement mend.
Learn mercy, now, from I who spare your life.
Show mercy that you failed to show your wife.
Enact my will in spirit and in form,
and you'll be blessed as you were here deformed."

Death's angel's index finger brushed his nose:

engulfed by darkness and its deepest throes.
Each sinew clenched with strength, to him, unknown.
His throat, closed off, he let out one last groan.
His bones, then, splintered like dry wooden beams.
His muscles split, like fabric, at their seams.
His eyes rolled back, detaching in their lair:
such pain awaits those who, defiant, err.

V

The King awoke, now purged of all his sin.
His bones ached not nor shifted 'neath his skin;
once more, his muscles fit their rightful mould;
his eyes saw clear each fold in Temple gold;
an inner peace prevailed and charged the air.
He rose, prepared to meet the world so fair.
He left, the veil restored and incense lit,
as magister of God's undoubted writ.

He longed to see the place where last she slept,
so finally, his loss he could accept.
As he approached the palace gates, men ran,
his absence had subsumed the house's plan.
Ignored he, shouts of joy at his return
and entered bower quiet for which he yearned.
Caressing red silk sheets, a tear drop fell.
But lo! An empty vial in her cell!

"What art thou?" asked the King of vial clear.
"Of Veisyan make.. yet all glass is, I fear...
Yet why would you beneath my wife's bed hide...?

29

I swear I've seen these marks upon the side...
Aha! This was Sengre's rare gift of sleep!
A gift to sneak a tool inside my keep?"
The King inquired at Sengre's whereabouts.
A peasant said: "Gone West; he is without."

"Then God, I pray, give me blue lightning's speed!
Let not fatigue approach my tireless steed!
An innocent or guilty man we chase:
the answer hid until we see his face.
Though fleeing in my weakest moment yet...
Better to stop him at the pass, I bet."
From thence, the thundering herd of hunters rode,
the Queen's late, wrongful death a leaden load.

Cross rivers blue and tree-filled vales they rode,
towards western pass hid in the mountain's bowed.
Three days they rode, pursuing faintest scents,
at times, washed off by streams, they came and went.
But four days out from high up Marquis' Pass,
the hounds a solid odor caught at last.
In two days time, pure eyesight could suffice:
they trapped the lords two hours from the heights.

Down to the dust they fell, upon their knees:
"Oh great, tremendous king of majesty,
we lay our case before your satin feet!
'Twas our vile wish to you, through lies, defeat.
We pried with gold and drink to set that scene,
portraying virtue chaste as longing mean.
Absolve us, please, of our most horrid acts

and pray, have mercy! Save us from the axe!"

While they pled this, the Priest and Southern Lord,
Sengre stood silent, hand upon his sword.
"Pathetic! Both!" he spat, "so quick to bow?
Confessing things you fail to apprehend!
Without my lead could ye have laid this snare?
And yet, you spill when struck by royal stare.
How know ye that he knows what we have done?
But now, our innocence is known to none!"

"You'll find my mood too sour for such lies,"
the King replied, "for this, you'll surely die.
These two, I spare: repentance earns such fare.
Your pride, however, lies beyond repair.
A hunch, I had, of your pernicious crimes,
yet pride's defense impeaches oftentimes:
you claim no guilt, yet from you malice flows
and leaves your motivations true exposed."

The two lost sheep rejoined the royal flock
in time becoming, for the Throne, two rocks.
And yet, Sengre's just death did not bring cheer
for he lamented still for his wife dear.
He wove artistic works with genius thread,
in mourning deep: an Office for the dead,
a ring of emerald, and golden rose.
Yet naught allayed or healed his somber woes...

Exhausting he all worldly avenues,
to God, he turned, to render him anew.

He ordered carved into the rock a tomb
compared to that to come, he hoped, her womb.
Her bier he adorned with roses red,
and to her final rest they slowly tread,
accompanied by those sweet songs he'd spun.
The King looked up: a white bird crossed the sun.

A Melody of Mud and Mysteries

LINDSEY ESSELMAN

I

A forceful torrent crashes from behind—
the air inside my lungs is jolted out,
as when I was a child, out of a tree
I fell, and now lay flat upon my back.
It's dark. My eyes are open, but it's dark.
My ears are ringing loud throughout my head.
I hear a thousand bells that call attention
to something I can't see and I can't hear.

As moments pass, my senses dull again.
The clouds that shroud my vision disappear.
I look down at my arms, my skin is mud:
a terracotta soldier, bathed in clay.
Beyond my arms, I see a mangled mess
of brown maroon with angles jutting out.
I recognize my own two legs and blood—

on sight, my stomach churns with chilling pain.

I raise my eyes and see a slope of mud,
my broken body slumped against the edge
of a crater on a cold and clammy moon.
Above me is a ring of dark'ning sky,
with sullen storm clouds casting down their shadows.
Rain fast approaches, blurring sky and earth,
and not far from where I lie indisposed,
a single plume of stony smoke swells up.

I hear a shot behind the crater wall,
and place and time come back to me at once.
In No Man's Land, the battle rages on,
a Friday morning, cheerless and alone.
The enemy so near—just to my left;
elusive safety somewhere to my right.
To stay here in-between would be to die;
to live, I must get up and move along.

I try to heave myself up to my feet—
my legs give out, I crumple to the ground.
So rolling over, now I'm lying prone,
and manage to drag forward just an inch,
another and again, to crater's edge.
I look around the flat expanse of gray,
but can't see the horizon through the rain.
My arms won't pull, my head drops down,
the pain and rain obscuring everything.

I can imagine the security

just yards away behind my brothers' lines.
It might as well be miles across the waves,
for I will never see that place again.
But now I see myself, as in a dream,
another body sunk in slime and sludge.
The rain embeds me in my prefab grave:
"From mud you are, to mud you shall return."

But open stay my eyes; I'm still alive,
by a strength not of myself, I cannot name.
And sudd'nly I'm aware of the small lump
beneath my chest, it sits inside my pocket.
A rosary of wood, my mother's once;
a weapon greater than a gun, she said.
Well now, the only weapon I have left
to fight the enemy when death draws near.

With all the strength I've left, my fingers move
to clutch the timeworn beads I've had of old,
not stiff, not harsh, like beads I've been supplied:
a cold hard string of metal balls and chains,
like bullets orderly and in a row.
As if of those I'd want my daily fill!
But no; instead, a softness and a warmth,
the wood worn where familiar fingers passed.

But one thing that, e'en now, sends chills to me,
above the well-loved crucifix of wood,
a bead in shape and likeness of a skull—
my fingers do not like to touch this one.
The sight, it irks me still, though I'm a man,

and after all the death I've seen up close.
But now's no time for doubts or second thoughts;
I must start now, or never pray again.

Before my rosary begins with Creed,
I once again become a child, and beg:
"If I should die before I wake, I pray
The Lord My soul to take." And so, with haste,
I start to pray the best I can with words:
"Almighty Father, in You I believe!"
I slide my fingers on to the next bead.
A hazy darkness covers both my eyes,
as I drift into a dark but wakeful sleep...

II

Until I see, in sudden turnabout,
a spirit of great beauty and resplendence,
with sword in hand, the other reaching out,
in robes of red and royal blue transcendence.
A golden light reflecting off his face:
a warmth that feels like sunset late in June,
the sunlight traveling through outer space,
and thrown back to the earth from shining moon.

My sight's obscured by gleaming radiant light,
the glory of some other world displayed!
I shield my dirty face in wondrous fright;
the figure speaks to me: "Don't be afraid!"
On my chest he puts his hand above my heart,
a smoky haze engulfs us on all sides,

and floating, flying upward soon we start,
on pure thin rushing air, we seem to glide.

And in no time the smoke begins to clear;
the dreamy dimness seems to vanish neatly,
revealing landscapes known to me so dear,
with rippling fields and finches chirping sweetly.
I recognize the dust and soybean leaves,
the red-brick school, the baseball field pass by,
as we, myself and Spirit, duck and weave,
maneuv'ring swiftly through the dusky sky.

The apple orchard comes into my view.
I see the ripened fruits of early fall,
but also, something different, something new;
I can't quite make it out; it's still too small—
"What's there?" I boldly ask my ghostly friend.
The spirit answers not, but draws me closer,
as from the sky we slightly do descend
until the orchard fair we're passing over.

I now can make out figures, shapes of men,
like stony statues gray in moonlight pale.
I wrack my brain, and try to comprehend;
who are these men, asleep, to no avail?
But my thoughts, they wander back to rustling trees,
imagining their shade in summer sun,
to lean against its base of strength and ease,
support against my back, fatigue undone.

But then my eyes alight upon another,

who's kneeling down, awake, his hands clasped tight
in prayer, his head bowed, as I now discover,
his mouth speaks words unheard into the night.
My angel brings me close enough to see
the drops of red that fall from forehead faint.
The fog clears up; I know who this must be!
It's Christ Himself, in my own hometown quaint!

The sweat of blood; it gave it all away.
"But what is going on? Why is He here?"
I ask my golden guide, in great dismay.
He answers not, but looks me sideways, queer,
and doubts crop up like sand burrs gone unseen
that send sharp prickles up my spine and neck.
What am I doing here? What does this mean?
I ask myself, as I fearfully reflect.

But my silent friend heeds not my new distress,
and upward to the sky again we go.
And, orchard leaving, onward we progress
through hazy air to dusty gravel road,
the one that skirts the town, a line of gold,
that leads into the fields of vivid green.
Along the way, far off, I now behold:
another crowd of men, another scene.

I see a darkened tree without leaf-span;
a figure's bound to it with leather ties.
As we get closer, I discern the man,
now barely man, disfigured and despised.
I catch my breath, my stomach lurches in.

With half-closed eyes I turn away and wince
as the men around take turns at scourging him,
whips cutting stripes into our censured Prince.

I look away, I can't take anymore.
No comfort in this dream now can I find!
"Kind Spirit, make it stop, please," I implore,
but he looks through me, as if he were blind.
"You see, don't you? This does no good to me!"
I shudder, almost wanting to wake up.
But from this dream I cannot yet be free,
and once again, we take our flight, abrupt.

III

This time, we're gliding just above the gravel,
so close, the crowd is right in front of us.
They move to let us through, and so we travel
toward the front, and closer to the fuss,
where Christ, the silent man, stands once again.
The dirt and sweat and blood cling to his limbs.
From somewhere far, I hear "Behold the man!"
The echoed words; a faint familiar hymn.

And in a flash I know what is to come,
as if I've known this place and time before.
More life-like than real life this dream's become;
behind my eyes I see the crown of thorns.
I try to disappear into the crowd,
forget the gruesome scene that haunts my vision.
But the spirit holds me fast, though bent and bowed,

to watch the progress of the King's derision.

The soldier men produce the piercing crown
and thrust it violently upon His head.
I'm close enough to see the blood drip down,
to wash the gravel underfoot in red.
A wooden reed they place into his hand,
with spit and scarlet robes they clothe him new.
I speak along with them, my words unplanned,
but somehow I say: "Hail, King of the Jews."

I hang my head; still, Spirit stands aloof.
Could this be punishment? Of course, it must.
A simple-seeming dream: now God's reproof.
"His suffering, on top of mine, for what?"
I ask, but yet expect no explanation.
With this the haze comes up. There is a blur—
which briefly makes me stifle my frustration.
As my head goes dizzy, landscapes tilt and whir.

The spirit pulls me onward down the road,
now leading out of town, and up the hill.
The hill I know so well; how it forebodes!
Atop which sits the solemn graveyard still.
The next unhappy mystery unfolds
as we walk that deadly, agonizing route.
And everything in detail, I behold
the smell of sweat and blood, the wails and shouts.

It hits me once again, that sacred sight!
Prepared I'll never be to catch a glimpse

of Christ Himself, the way, the truth, the light,
but now he's doubled over as he limps.
The wood digs in his shoulders, and each step
is slower than the last, as is each breath.
He struggles, stumbling, stooping to the depths
of a criminal deserving brutal death.

So up the hill we go, and next I hear
the pounding sound as nails drive through his hands.
It staggers me—oh, make it disappear!
And heedlessly, they raise the Son of Man.
The sun is low, its glare is hot and bright.
Three trees upon a hill, a common scene;
but to me, it seems to be the darkest night,
and these three trees are not all that they seem.

And without warning, Spirit leaves my side.
The crowd around me dimly fades to nothing.
A darkness falls upon the countryside—
uphill I raise my eyes, my face is flushing.
As I look upon the cross, from which light sweeps,
a soft but dazzling gleam of glorious gold,
not harsh, not sharp, but penetrating deep,
to touch the soul, its mysteries untold.

I find the face of Christ within the rays—
his eyes meet mine, my trembling knees give out.
I fall to them; I cannot look away,
and I know he won't; he never will, no doubt!
The stretch of time and space, but only him.
A hundred billion souls, but only me.

And yesterday means naught, the past grows dim;
this is today; eternal day, I see!

And, swelling in my eyes, the tears come now,
as I look into his, amazed and awed.
The grief, the joy, the peace, the pain... but how?
How can he feel these passions, he who's God?
How can they drive him to these drastic lengths,
for our sake, my sake? He, my debt to pay,
to die this way, with shame, instead of strength?
It overwhelms me, I must look away.

IV

And when I look back up, the scene is gone.
No hill, no cross, the darkness swallows all.
I look around in fear, the dream goes on,
and in the empty darkness I feel small.
Until a beam of light appears, agleam,
approaching me, a woman dressed in white.
Who, coming closer, reaches out to me,
intense and clear like sun, her eyes shine bright.

And straightaway, collapsing in her arms,
the tears of flooding warmth stream down my face.
For here I know I will not come to harm,
defended by a mother's warm embrace.
She doesn't have to say a single word,
but pulls me nearer, holds me close and tight.
Her touch is soft, the fine wings of a bird.
As she strokes my face, her gentle hand is light.

So after fleeting time of sweet repose,
I look up to her shining eyes, and ask,
"What next should I do? What do you propose?
What work of mine could be a worthy task?
I've seen his vast compassion, perfect, true,
and nothing now can matter or compare;
no fight, nor toil, nor labor, can I do.
Don't send me back again to be ensnared."

She turns her gaze to me with tender eyes.
"An angel came to visit me once, too.
At first it troubled me, destabilized
the whole world, everything I ever knew.
'Be not afraid!' the angel bold decreed,
as he revealed the Christ-child's incarnation:
fruit of my womb and blest fruit of the tree,
on whose worn wood will hang our sweet salvation.

"Now don't deceive yourself or be mistaken;
at first I did not know what words to say.
For when I heard this news, I was quite shaken,
but I knew God must do with me what he may.
And when it came my dearest son's dark time
to give the blood-bought gift of our redemption,
his suffering and sorrow were all mine,
and the world's were his, united in perfection.

"But even now, just moments past, you've seen
the modern fears and failures taken up.
All ancient, and all new, our sins washed clean,
by sacrifice of Christ's unpassing cup.

But he doesn't leave us here to go astray.
To imitate his ways: commands he this,
that we obtain his promise every day,
the offering that brings eternal bliss!"

"Obtain his holy promise every day"—
I realize its meaning, for my sake.
My future and my present: here they lay,
in front of me, the truth: I must awake!
This dream world's real, but so's the waking world,
and there are things in it that must be done;
so with the sail of prayer at last unfurled,
I'll suffer, but I'll know the battle's won.

I look once more to see her face gold-rimmed,
for I know this wondrous sleep comes to a close.
As she smiles at me, her light begins to dim.
This is the trying moment, I suppose,
when on my journey home I must set out,
to use, remember, practice what I've learned.
But harder than it seems, to be devout—
to stay with her forever, still I yearn.

"Please stay here, Mother, don't leave me just yet!"
I cry to her, though I know it's in vain.
The stress of waking brings me to a sweat,
as I remember all the grief and pain
that waits for me in battle, dark and dreary.
"Remember, my dear son," she says to me,
"the promises of Christ when you get weary."
And with those words she turns and starts to flee.

I watch her disappear into the dark,
and this time, I'm aware, it is for good.
For a moment brief my hopes again look stark.
I long to stay here still; I wish I could!
My head feels fuzzy, like it did before,
my body, absent, distant, sinking deep,
my thoughts unclear— can't think straight anymore,
and once again I'm blanketed by sleep.

V

My eyes are slow and strenuous to open,
to see the dull gray mass I left behind.
But now I'm back, immersed again, awoken,
to carry out the earthly hack and grind.
As I look around me, inwardly I groan.
The ache and throb of cold, wet wounds return.
And on and on, the noise of battle drones,
the trial of bullets never to adjourn.

I hearken back the pleasant memories
of just a moment past, my lovely dream!
For now this dream recalls a treasury
of joys and comforts, bursting at the seams.
But even now, in such a short time hence,
the images are fading by and by.
My backdrop bleak becomes more real, I sense.
The doubts begin to tug: was it a lie?

I shudder, bring my hands up to my face;
then noticing the beads that lie therein—

the rosary! Well, this resolves the case.
The vision-dream legitimate had been.
I clasp, caress my wooden beads and think:
the orchard trees, the post, the crown, the cross—
are right here in my hands, in wooden links.
Without this prayer, I'm sure all would be lost.

Upon another survey close, I see
a striking sight, though not unfortunate:
the eerie skull that used to rattle me,
and send me chills, I do not now forget.
But this time when I see its curious grin,
I'm not afraid, for Christ has conquered death.
Instead I see a warning: "Do not sin!
But trust in him for every waking breath."

And with this trust, I fold my hands to pray:
"Remember Lord, your creature, who, in blood,
you have redeemed today and every day.
Deliver me, like Noah, from the flood,
and grant the daily pittance of your grace
to overcome temptation weak and strong.
Do not let me despair or quit the race
until the day I join in heaven's song."

My strength renewed, I know what I must do:
to safety I must run, or walk, or crawl.
With grunts and groans I will my limbs to move,
and slow, with gritted teeth, I pull and haul
up through the mucky, ever-present sand.
I slowly rise upon my freezing feet,

and quaking like a newborn fawn, I stand,
with mind made up: my journey I'll complete.

I look around and see the barren trees
and stagnant pools of rotten murky scum.
For miles, no color, charm, or warming breeze,
the flat expanse goes on to kingdom come.
I upward turn my head toward the sky
as raindrops start to pelt my dirty face.
I let them wash the crust and grime good-bye;
refreshment of my spirit takes their place.

A ways away, I see the sharpened wires
that mark the territory of my line.
I trudge to that elusive place, inspired,
with fierce determination, all divine.
The going's slow but steady. I proceed,
each step becoming quicker than the last.
And inch by inch, I look ahead to see—
I stop abruptly, catch my breath and gasp!

On low horizon sits a golden band,
where blue and purple streaks and smudges glow.
The sun breaks through the clouds and lights the land:
a heav'nly blaze bestowed on us below.
I scan the skyline, taking in the thrill,
and gazing at the scene, my mind's at ease.
Behind my lines stands up a hazy hill;
there sit the silhouettes of three tall trees.

A smile breaks through, excitement fills my chest.

In haste, I limp along, my eyes transfixed.
Of all imagination, this is best;
in joyfulness, all anguish is eclipsed!
Around me howitzers and mortars sound,
through deepest, darkest valley where I roam.
Come sword, come missile, come, rain hellfire down!
Not one can hurt me: I am going home!

A Fighter and her Typewriter

EVITA PILAR DUFFY-ALFONSO

I

By night she faced the growling beasts and creeps,
a haunting of the demons while she sleeps.
The morning light she hoped would bring her ease,
her clammy hands not cured by morning breeze.
She brushes off the horrors of the night
by mindlessly ignoring mind and fright.
She does not think to pray for sanity;
Concha did not know Christianity.

The Saco family did not believe:
"A God was meant for only the naïve."
The patriarch was an Enlightened man;
he was no fool and followed his own plan.
The Church, he blamed, for snubbing worldly wisdom;
in Spain, less God, would make the perfect system.

Unhappy and quite empty she was then;
Concha could not take one more dream again.

Her mother was no intellectual;
she did not think of death eventual.
Her mind absorbed in only what she saw,
and grandchildren from her daughter was law.
Her heart so yearned for wedding bells and veils,
and primes Concha with matrimony tales.
She set her daughter up with single males;
her daughter hated them with no details.

A book, a play, a date were never fun;
she was unsatisfied with everyone.
She needed more than all the courting guys—
a kind of being who has seeing eyes.
Concha did not understand all of that;
she had never read from the *Magnificat*.
Her education was pure secular;
her grasp of truth was fairly cellular.

She walked on weekends to the city stores;
her mother wanted groceries outdoors.
Concha, while walking across Madrid, thought:
"My life is nightmares, plus the daily naught."
Along the cobblestone she took a pause;
ethereal deep voices were the cause.
She heard the ancient hymnals Marian
and loved these songs by seminarians.

A blessing was Concha was not alone;

her cousin was a priest who lived in Rome.
Her cousin, Juan, was studying to be
a servant of the holy One-in-Three.
That day she wrote to him confusingly:
"Is Christ now beckoning me musically?"
He sent her books in only a few weeks:
a Bible and "lives of the saints" she keeps.

On patron saint of Spain she gaily read,
but cried when she heard of the way Christ bled.
The stories of the saints she learned in shock
for all of their spirits were like a rock.
The story of Saint Paul she loved the most—
conversion was done by the Holy Ghost.
Devouring each tale of bravery,
she saw her soul was bound in slavery.

Concha's most useful talent for her quest
is that of gifted writer. She was blest.
Indeed, it was not very long before
the girl was writing lots of saintly gore.
Deciding to become more like the saints,
she throws away all wicked world constraints.
With reading and her writing she became
a saintly model among the mundane.

In secret she converted at the church—
the one whose song began her holy search.
The night after she ate the bread of life,
her dreams were finally free from all strife.
She thinks of all the Catholics who died,

of how they sacrificed their homes and lives.
A thousand were willing to die for Christ,
so telling her parents was a small price.

She told her parents of her faith in God
and how she wants to be a nun of frod.
Concha's dear father was taken aback:
"Is reason in my daughter quite this lack?"
Her mother fell into hysteria:
their home was a disaster area.
Despite Concha finally having peace,
the testing of her faith was yet to cease.

II

There lived a joyful man around that time.
"I love my wife and life," he'd often chime.
One every morning, his day job would call,
so dutifully José never stalled.
On weekday mornings when he left his home,
his wife sprinkled the water blessed in Rome.
His life was full of love and perfection,
but God had planned another direction.

In early marriage tragedy became
the reason he smashed every picture frame.
His youthful wife became pregnant with twins;
in childbirth, all three met seraphim.
Despair consumed the painfully sad man.
He looked to heaven: "God, is this your plan?"
He did not know of any way to cope,

and mad with Christ, he had no sense of hope.

No longer could one friend see him so blue:
"Arranged marriage would surely help him through."
His friend had other things he aspired for.
Yes, there were other private goals in store:
When offering Concha, he hoped she would
abandon hopes of holy sisterhood.
Concha was plagued with vocational woe;
her father's wishes were a dreadful blow.

Concha had not known God too long at all,
and adhered to her parents' worldly call.
She sometimes wondered of a different path,
but choices grounded her in aftermath.
She married José, easing most his pain,
but she could never supplant his first dane.
With little passion they lived happily,
for they were bonded over family.

and José found some consonance,
the Lord a sense of Godliness.
d had brought him to the light,
to know Christ.
hing the faith
daith.
wake,
would bake.

nstruction
tion.

Her oldest son was elementary age,
but never felt he was put in a cage.
In catechisms, she knew all the excerpts;
she soon became a Catholic expert.
She was a holy intellectual,
so all her lessons were effectual.

Her children learned of Joel and Hosea
and prayed: *"Dios te salve, Maria."*
She told the children of the convert Saul
before each one of them made their first crawl.
With typewriter and nightly time to spare,
she taps each key with eloquence and care.
She writes of her beloved Catholic faith
to publish beside partisans and scathe.

One evening, she got some scary mail;
a note from her priest cousin made her pale.
He warned of anti-Catholicism,
a cause of burgeoning communism.
While serving his historic Seville church,
he saw all political violence lurch.
He urged she seek adequate protection
before the soon upcoming election.

She rushed to José: "Let us get away!"
But José said his family would stay.
"My job is what provides us everything."
She argued but recalled her wedding ring.
Concha promised her husband deference
and agreed to follow his preference.

She knew he looked out for their livelihood
and devoted her thoughts to Motherhood.

Yet worrisome notes from her cousin brought
Concha anxiety and overwrought.
Her husband said there may be division,
but Spain would never turn on religion.
She shifted her writing from the divine
to focus on competing party lines.
If she can't leave Madrid, then she will write.
The ink and paper are her way to fight.

III

The news was filled with bloody articles;
the headlines told of murdered cardinals.
The convents were not safe for holy nuns.
They raped them before pulling out their guns.
She shivered while walking past every mirror.
If she had taken vows, she'd share their horror.
Absorbed in perpetual news of death,
her haunting dreams repeated her last breath.

Her husband worried if he'll lose his Job.
Poor José deeply feared the Marxist mob.
Concha knew José was consumed in worry.
She wanted to leave Madrid in a hurry.
He wanted to first have a careful getaway.
"Oh, God, let us please stay," he'd often pray.
Concha only had articles she wrote.
The Popular Front cancelled out her vote.

Soon José was quite frequently harassed
because he was Catholic and middle-class.
A family friend who would never tell lies
informed José to watch out for the spies.
A fearful José was truly concerned;
arrest would mean he never would return.
For many of his friends had disappeared,
and on the streets—dead—they would reappear.

A letter brought the family scary news,
and for Concha it was the final fuse.
Concha's dear cousin Juan was executed.
She burst in tears: "Why are we persecuted?"
To save her kids they needed to escape.
They would not die by Madrid's leftist rape.
That moment she began to make her plans.
No one would harm her sleeping little lambs.

At that same time José met his good friend,
who frantically warned him: "This is the end!
You need to hide. For you they are coming.
If they find you, just never stop running!"
His whole being was swallowed up in fear;
his spinning mind would not let him think clear.
"I found him!" José heard, and then he ran,
just like all of the Spanish clergymen.

He did not run home toward his kids and wife,
for they would slaughter the lights of his life
He dashed through Madrid's narrow streets and slid.
A jagged stone made José do a skid.

The Marxist were able to apprehend
a man facing a truly bitter end.
Arrested now, José looks Innermost:
"Prepare my soul for death, O Holy Ghost!"

When José fails to return home that night,
Concha thinks this must be a night for flight.
A note arrives in cold and pouring rain,
delivering to her a horrid pain.
She learns beloved José was taken,
so now she and her kids are forsaken.
She looks upon her precious babes sleeping;
she know there is no time for more weeping.

She hopes José is only sent to jail.
The worst they'd do is make him cold and frail.
She understands that José could be killed,
exactly why she must remain strong-willed.
Her husband had a rural family strain,
who live in the safety of Northern Spain.
She will go to their haven from the war
and wait out all the horrifying gore.

To sneak away she knows she can not pack;
she must only take what fits on her back.
She woke the four of her kids together
and bundled them up for the winter weather.
A photograph of her husband reminds
Concha she's leaving everything behind.
She took what's crucial as mom and writer:
her four babes, and her trusty typewriter.

Their slender shadows cast by bright starlight,
she takes the children on a train at midnight.
They headed to Franco territory.
One day, she prayed, he'd restore Spain's glory.
For now, she gave thanks that they all survived;
her four little angels were still alive.
She told her frightened kids of Noah's Ark,
and "Jesus is wherever we embark."

IV

All that Concha knew in her life was gone
as she came to Salamanca at dawn.
At journey's end, Concha was drained and frozen,
just like the Virgin when she birthed the Chosen.
In early morn, Concha faced her in-laws.
Not seeing José, made their feelings raw.
With no son in sight, José's mom had fears,
and when Concha confirmed she burst in tears.

The children were already petrified.
Because of grandma's sob, they also cried.
Concha tried to make the small ones feel whole.
She could not cure the distress in their souls.
Yet ultimately the whole family wept,
for José's dreadful fate they could not accept.
Then José's father said, "We are not harmed.
Let us give thanks and focus on the farm."

The following weeks brought Concha great stress.
The worry wouldn't let her decompress.

She looked for solace in the daily Mass
and saw the righteous saints in bright stained glass.
As Joan of Arc drew her great silver sword,
Concha thought, "I need back my vocal chord."
Near mighty Joan, Concha felt powerless.
"If I can't write, I fall to cowardice."

If she can't show the world what she can write,
then she was not even part of the fight.
She had to worry about getting food;
the war effort left little for her brood.
Concha feared they'd succumb to starvation.
The nation was lost, with no salvation.
Her mind astray and alarmingly dark
because she missed the family patriarch.

She reads about the horrors of the war
and feels of no help with her mundane chores.
She knows across the country churches burn
for religion they wanted overturned.
The streets ran red with priest's and nun's blest blood,
their bodies cast in giant pits of mud.
They needed holy devotion to rot,
so that they could fulfill the Marxist plot.

Concha's days were always quite repetitious,
and she became overly unambitious.
The nightmares have come back to haunt her sleep;
because of them she often wakes and weeps.
By stories of war she was impacted,
and all day long Concha was distracted.

She felt how she did before knowing God,
but for her children she had a façade.

The work she does is ineffectual;
no more is she an intellectual.
"No one cares if my typing is biting.
There's none alive to read all my writing.
It does not matter if I am trying;
all of my Spanish people are dying."
In all these tragic thoughts she was consumed.
All people of faith were doomed, she assumed.

One day in Holy Mass she hears from God
and realizes her thinking has been flawed.
As soon as she opened her heart and prayed,
her drained and hallowed soul was set ablaze.
It's like her favorite tale of holy Paul;
the Spirit overwhelmed her, and she bawled.
The whole church seems to fill with heaven's light,
and she sees her crucial role in the fight.

At home she tells the children a saint story;
she'd forgotten to tell tales for God's glory.
She told the kids how Saul fell off his horse
and how the Holy Spirit changed his course.
Concha's tale made each child very raptured,
in awe of Paul's great faith after his capture.
Her kids remind her of her conversion
and how she wanted holy submersion.

She hears her kids pray in God's brilliance,

for Him to grant their father resilience.
They also pray for God to bring him back
and deliver José from out the black.
She sees in little faces all her hope;
her job is their faith, so she should not mope.
She thanks the Lord for giving salvation;
she can do good despite her location.

V

Now back to José in the war's great craze,
after he had been taken for long days.
For three years he lived in a makeshift cell
where he was sentenced unfairly to dwell.
The proceeding of his initial trial
ran by a jury that was hostile.
He was not locked alone and shared his jail
with one neighborhood priest and two more males.

He tried recalling his little kid's faces
and constantly was asking God for graces.
One day in maddening dark and damp prison,
his dreams displayed him a heavenly vision.
"Oh do not fear," said the unearthly wraith,
"for Christ will save you and restore the faith."
So José did not lose hope for three years,
and internal prayers gave him true cheer.

At war's end, all his old cell mates were shot—
a cruel end to the Marxist's thwarted plot.
But José managed to escape and runs.

If he were to stop, he'd die by their guns.
He only can see victorious troops;
they are all part of General Franco's group.
He sees Our Lady of Pillar and cries;
he gives great thanks with his hands to the skies.

In safety he runs back to his old house
to frantically look for his kids and spouse.
When he arrived he was met with a scare,
for many strangers were residing there.
He tried to remove the entitled scum;
they would not return to where they came from.
He could not find his family anywhere
and subsequently fell into a scare.

Concha was also looking for her love;
the whole way home she prayed to God above.
When she saw how once great Madrid was torn,
Concha felt far more exhausted and worn.
The church where she first heard the holy tunes
was pillaged and became nothing but ruins.
All she could do is hold her small ones tight;
she praised the Lord her children were alright.

They were reunited by a close friend,
and their separation came to an end.
The family met on top of all the rubble,
and in many tears of joy each one crumbled.
Concha and José saw that each had aged;
they lost much while the dreadful war had raged.
Yet not one of them was a little hateful,

for living they were eternally grateful.

Concha learns the deed to their house is lost;
they are sadly cast out into the frost.
The Marxists took all of their costly things,
yet all together they felt just like kings.
For refuge the family prayed a Hail Mary,
and were granted it from the military.
The family was bestowed a place to stay,
and for that they all bowed their heads and prayed.

In war, the church goers had been booted,
and all the church's contents were looted.
After the faithful faced to Marxist bull,
the holy Easter Mass was still quite full.
The faithful had to perform Mass outside.
Concha's heart swelled with Spanish, Catholic pride.
Their Easter candles withstood the cold air.
They now shared communion most anywhere.

At supper the family looks much thinner;
they were excited to share a dinner.
They had no lamb, so they had to eat chicken.
For now the family is poverty stricken.
Yet they still perform the sign of the cross.
They trust in God despite all of their loss.
Concha tells all the children to be cheerful.
After enduring war, they can't be fearful.

In later years, Concha wrote a kids' book,
which made many catch on Christ's holy hook.

It was filled with the saintly tales she told—
the ones that made her kids blessed and bold.
Her legacy was not the typewritten;
instead, she was known for the unwritten.
She produced deeply devout descendants
that turned into her greatest remembrance.

Alma Mater

CONRAD MOJICA

I

Straight from the east a harsh chill wind did rush;
the winter's leaves dried up and blew away.
The town's main road hid underneath the slush,
reflected by a sky completely gray;
surrounding forests' widespread underbrush
enveloped by a snow as hard as clay.
The withered field of wheat displays a sign:
"Welcome to Alma—the Midwest's pipeline."

There, donned in black, stood Alma's favorite son
amongst the intimate Midwestern swarm.
Approaching Walter, speaking one-by-one,
the group's collective heat kept Walter warm.
Crowd members with the exception of none
shared Walter's black ensemble as the norm.

Although all stand prepared in Sunday best,
they are waiting on just one final guest.

At last, appearing out in the distance,
a shining, black vehicle of great price
sped toward them with visible persistence
that drifts around deadly hazards of ice.
The dirt kicked up and formed a consistence
of filth on the surface made to entice.
The Tesla's rims' slow spin was hypnotic
to all the people's eyes, so exotic.

The door swung open, revealing a man.
The once-buzzing small town's people fell mute.
His leather seats matched his most recent tan;
his jet-black hair matched his Armani suit.
The crowd knew not who stood before the clan,
when suddenly he gave the town's salute.
They knew now, looking at one another—
it was Jacob: Walter's only brother.

All of the crowd's gaze moved to Walter's eyes
which recognized Jacob coming from farms.
He beamed with daybreak's light and great surprise:
"Well, Jacob, you made it!" Walter alarms.
"I'm happy to be back here," Jacob lies.
Walter approached him with his outstretched arms.
Jacob looked at his grizzled, childish face
and exchanged an awkward, foreign embrace.

They're now complete, the crowd began to march

a familiar path they all had gone before.
All of their knuckles were as white as starch
as they walked by the three remaining stores.
They passed below the leaning oak's great arch
lockstep, as if they were headed to war.
Yet the destination of their great quest
was to lay one of their most loved to rest.

At last, they came upon the rusted gate
at the oldest of their town's locations.
They formed a circle, with hearts full of weight
and filed to their respective stations
as if it was each individual's fate,
and stood on grounds of past generations.
The two somber brothers were side by side
without even touching, their thoughts collide.

This place always reminded them of dad
and how he would speak with brimstone and fire.
The immense sway over crowds that he had
with his sermons as he would perspire,
never stopping once to look at his pad.
In their grief, his eulogies would inspire.
Both of their stares were unbearably bleak
as the newest pastor began to speak.

His sermon quite cliché, the pastor stressed:
"God works in most mysterious of ways."
A timid man, not speaking with his chest,
he brought the brothers' minds back to a haze.
In Walter's mind: "This is not Alma's best."

In Jacob's mind: "He will go on for days."
They exchanged mirrored expressions of fraught.
"This job was supposed to be Dad's," both thought.

Next, bearers lift the pall up to the sky—
a coffin heavy, distinguished, and browned.
They whisper to Walter, to no reply.
Circling the hole, they gathered around
with all wondering why good people die
as the coffin was lowered to the ground.
The group then prayed the twenty-seventh Psalm
as the two brothers parted with their mom.

II

They sit in the cafeteria now
of Trinity Lutheran, its known air stale.
And grazing the section's buffet like cows,
the townsfolk mill around, gentle and frail.
Walter concentrates and furrows his brow;
Jacob darts his eyes and picks at his nail.
Each brother with muted grief in his heart;
they sit beside each other, miles apart.

Their mom's best friend comes with lilies lilac.
She hugs both with a face streaming of tears.
But then she smiles and produces a stack
of photos dating back to childhood years.
As they look through the prints, Walter chats back
while brother Jacob mostly looks and hears.
Despite this, smiles and laughter both are shared.

They come together; memories repaired.

As photos pass, everyone grows older.
Their first of Christmases without their dad;
the latter years, how Walter consoled her;
Mom with Walter's trade school's small class of grads;
in her wheelchair now as Walter rolled her;
by her bedside with both expressions glad.
Jacob saw memories that weren't his own
and uncontrolled his mind began to roam.

He looked around his alma mater
and mused how all there present shared the same.
They send their kids, their sons and daughters;
old teachers look for familiar surnames.
They line them up, like pigs for slaughter
and praise the tradition, a noble aim.
And in those halls, children meet friends for life.
They find their future husband, future wife.

He quickly realized on a short breath:
all town's funerals also ended here.
Reception at school following a death.
Someone's liver drowned by a life of beer;
someone's brain rotted by his crystal meth.
Another year, a death, another year.
Indiscriminate ends with just one rule:
all go down at Trinity Lutheran school.

Taking all of this in, his mind now raced.
Within a town whose motto: "Why mettle?"

Your dreams are dreams, intended not to chase.
Alma is the perfect place to settle.
Now lay all your ambitions down to waste.
You blooming flowers, now drop your petals.
Don't you know that outside the hometown fort,
the life of man: nasty, brutish, and short?

For Alma's old, life stamped and signed and sealed.
And now he knew this fate belongs to Mom.
Perplexed at what could possibly appeal,
her last years spent 'round medicine and balm,
what could she have gotten out of the deal?
Or why Dad, who dropped his sermons like bombs,
would shirk chances to fly the chicken coop,
instead opting for aging, shrinking groups?

It was just too much for his mind to bear.
He wished not to think of lives going down.
He thought of New York: it's much nicer there.
He looked at the tables near him and frowned.
He thought, as he looked out windows and stared,
"The rented car will take me back to town.
I'll bring it back and take a direct flight.
If I head out now, I'll be back tonight."

She left them now, sharing a final cry.
Walter then noticed Jacob's longing gaze—
a face so flushed, with wild, bewildered eyes.
He looked like prophets who speak tongues in praise.
Walter tried waving hands to no reply.
At last, he spoke to interrupt the haze.

"Jacob," said Walter, "would you like a word?
I'm here for you; now let your speech be heard."

Not wanting to talk things within this vein,
Jacob, now removed, instinctive objects.
But looking at Walter, he felt a pain—
not knowing its origins, distressed, perplexed.
Then he realized, racking all his brain:
first dad, now mom: he knew Walter was next.
But Walter was young! His future not locked.
"Walter," said Jacob, "let's go for a walk."

III

The two echoed their stomping on the floor
as they now roamed the hallway's small expanse.
They both knew not what Jacob had in store.
At times, the puzzled Walter sneaks a glance
to start a conversation, yet ignored.
Impenetrable Jacob caught in trance.
In lockstep, neither followed, neither led.
Naught understood, and not a word was said.

The halls enveloped the two men in black;
the rushing wind made windows shake and ache.
The peeling pastel plaster walls were cracked,
and trials of paper scattered in the wake
on paths to doors which stand way in the back
when children fled last week for Christmas break.
A couple rusty lockers left ajar
when Alma schoolboys rushed to mother's car.

They turned the corner, instantly they stopped,
magnificent tall lockers causing halt.
Conjoined in glory, scanned by both like hawks,
determined both to search for newest faults.
The gleaming black façade, the double locks,
resembling less a locker, more a vault.
The silver logos gleamed like precious gems.
They stood just how the brothers had left them.

The hush was broken, grinning ear to ear
was Walter, "Recall these were yours and mine?
When we would walk the halls to our friends' cheers?
I bet the inside door still has my sign.
We ran this school for all those many years,
and look! These lockers also aged like wine!
I loved it when we'd walk onto the bus,
and everyone wanted to sit by us."

His brother snorted: "Twenty years ago.
Our childhood social status. You still care?
I could not be further from that time. Although
we can look at old photos—that is fair—
you can't go back and need to learn to grow.
We are men, and you speak of youth. I swear,
our childhood years do not decide our caste.
Must you entirely live back in the past?"

His words made Walter's face now flush with red,
but he stayed calm and kept anger at bay.
"From past to present, my life can be thread
through my relationships here, like crochet.

: be shed,
e today.
you,
h and through.”

e

e!

e,

n,

n,

birthed

n,

rth.

s

ayed.
unt.

eth”

,
erse);

Said Walter, "We've put our gifts to good ends;
by 'nothing' I'm not quite sure what you mean
I have a well-kept home, amazing friends,
and have worked very hard for every cent.
True, I do not have a Tesla or Benz;
In any case, I am to be content.
In Alma, I'm proud of what I achieve.
Apologies, I'm not going to leave."

IV

"Walter, with money Dad did not leave muc
but he gave us our talents to produce.
When he passed, I needed to come in clutc
so I escaped here and put them to use,
on top of all my field, keeping in touch
with markets and the news, never obtuse.
I traveled all the corners of the earth
And tenfold, I finally grew my worth.

"Of talents, he gave you the same amount
But, cautious Walter, you then were afraic
of global challenges you must surmount.
You feared all of these risks, and so you st
You stashed your talent deep in your accc
I see now clearly, you cannot be swayed.
Go, keep your talents buried underneath
and look forward to weeping gnashing te

These words of Jacob took Walter aback
(most surprised Jacob still could recite v

his temper and restraint began to crack.
His life was better, Jacob's life was worse.
So done with hearing him and cutting slack,
with Jacob's witless attempts to coerce.
He looked at his brother's confident face,
deciding it time to put him in place.

"Oh, Jacob, all your success sits on sand:
you live with no foundation. Yes, for now,
enjoy your position of high demand.
You've held on to it for this long, somehow.
But Jacob, ask yourself: will this house stand
when streams do rise and rain comes pouring down?
Unraveling occurs, your house is struck
because all that you have is built on luck.

"What I have here is settled on the rock,
the product I have worked for all my life,
It's patience and results with little talk.
And when encountering a pain or strife,
I have my support all throughout my block.
My simple world here is completely rife
with joy. I live by doing what I love
and am always at peace with God above."

"You seriously think that this is luck?
I persistently knocked on every door.
You don't perceive my plans that ran amuck
and all the things that I've had to ask for.
All those intricate bargains that I've struck
and all the hours into my work I've poured.

The importunate neighbor is my name;
I get what I want, and I have no shame.

"Yes, Walter, you possess a mental block.
You claim to follow the way of the wise,
yet you remain too proud yourself to knock.
Allow, if you don't mind, me to surmise:
you're jealous of me, but can only mock
and keep yourself going off of your lies.
Now take off your ego-covered dark mask;
in order to receive, you must first ask."

"You're no neighbor, you're a prodigal son
who left your family when needed most.
You say, 'I'll do New York! Alma's no fun.
I've wealth, excitement, and success to boast,
of household obligations I have none.'
You fled and coldly abandoned your post.
You checked in once a year, having the gall
to push our mom off the phone in your calls.

"I'm sure you enjoyed dining with the pigs,
ignoring us, thinking your hands are cleansed.
And taking advantage of systems rigged.
You kept in touch? Perhaps you did—with trends.
Your luck will run out; you won't find a gig,
but it will be too late to make amends:
no mother or father to kill the calf,
only the older brother, who will laugh."

This time, Jacob offered no more response.

Instead, he stared at him with empty eyes.
The halls were brought to silence all at once,
remained with no more subjects to discuss.
The sadness deep in Walter's heart that haunts
him quickly multiplied double in size.
He knew not what from this talk had been gained
besides further distance, furthermore pain.

V

"My brother," Jacob at last said, "speaks the truth.
How can I say that you live in the past,
when I am the one so wrapped up in youth?
You nursed, while I lived unconcerned and fast;
I drove the car while you paid the tollbooth.
Now I see this meeting will be our last,
for it's too late now for me to atone.
I lost my family, fate carved in stone.

"Now orphans for the rest of all our days.
Most orphans never get to know their folks.
God gave 18 years with Dad, who amazed,
and 18 more with Mom, strong as an oak.
Ignoring His great gift, not giving praise,
and half those years avoiding them like hoax.
They gave me the best life that they could give,
while I treated them like lost relatives."

Here Jacob spoke in short and sobbing breaths,
but Walter then embraced him like a child.
Forgiveness provided the shibboleth

which caused Jacob's extensive grief to mild.
They walked away from the shadow of death
and veered to outside doors walking in file.
Both doors were opened with collective push;
onto their faces, rays of light now rushed.

The sky had cleared and now was sapphire blue.
The silver river gave a mighty roar.
The conifers gave off emerald hue.
A pair of ruby birds flew up and soared.
Was this the Alma Jacob thought he knew?
The sight unlocked the memories he stored
of days spent in the sun, nights starry eyed—
in each, Walter was always by his side.

"Look, Jacob, we're the only blood we've got.
Our mom and dad are gone, so we've been told.
We have our work set out for us. We ought
to support each other throughout this cold.
I'm rooting for you to sweeten your pot
and increase your talents one hundred-fold.
In Alma, I will yet continue still:
our mom and dad have quite big shoes to fill."

"Without you, Walter, we all would be cursed.
Our mother lived those years due to your care.
You do embody her, twice reinforced:
so steadfast and loyal, all pacts fulfilled,
while never failing your family first,
the rock upon which all of us are built.
I am not worthy to be called your friend;

you need not olive branches to extend."

"But Jacob, on yourself do not be down.
I took your message of New York quite bad
as no prophet's accepted in his town.
You say that I am Mom; well, you are Dad:
with infinite potential all around,
just using Alma as a launching pad.
Nevertheless, the difference that you've got
is that you truly went where he could not."

"If what we say is true," Jacob began,
"then perhaps mother and father do live.
Our life is a race that we've barely ran.
To one another, we've a lot to give."
"Now that they are done with their own life span,"
said Walter, "we must learn how to forgive.
Together, we can do what others could.
It is time to restore our brotherhood."

At the end the two went their separate ways.
Now both possessed a rebuilt state of mind,
intent on setting both their worlds ablaze.
They spoke always, their vacations aligned;
for their next kin they showed the path they paved.
Without their parents, fates were intertwined.
They'll live apart but stand on the same ground.
The brothers both were lost, but now they're found.

You'll look down on where you came from sometimes,
but you'll always have this place to call home.

None of our stories stay within the lines;
we stay, we go; despite how far we roam
in our origin's eyes, we all keep our shine.
All are welcomed back to God's great Kingdom.
May our own hearts be our best choice of judge,
and may we live our lives without a grudge.

Musings and Visions of a Birdkeeper's Son

JACQUES REYNOIR

I

An eagle soars high up above the ground,
glides North and South throughout the heaven's skies.
The golden beak in front guides him around.
His wings and feathers reach far out lengthwise.
A gander underneath his sight had found;
another world lies distant from his eyes.
He watches high a garden far from throw,
a world of birds and Keeper down below.

As father feeds the card'nals and the jays,
I spot a sovereign eagle's lofty height.
"Look up," I scream and point at what I gaze.
"There flies an eagle swift through wind in flight."
Confused, Birdkeeper's eyes had skyward raised.
He did not find the grand bird within sight.
"I see no godly bird in our dimension.

I deem it must have been your mind's invention."

Birdkeeper claimed a subtle gift of old,
from times of Odin of Germania.
He understood the language the birds told,
and spread the word at House Octavia.
He lures the birds with food the feeder holds
that brings the birds to state of mania.
Ethnicities of birds are brought to war,
addicted to the wicked seeds in store.

The first are card'nals born of feather red,
who sing together through each waking day.
Their feeder neighbor whom they have most dread:
the rude, obnoxious, boisterous blue jay.
"I wish those vexing blue jays to be dead!
They interrupt our song and stop our play.
But worst of all they pose a mighty threat,
to steal the sweetened seed that feeder set."

The blue jays rival card'nals at the feeder,
their banter captivating all the time.
With chatter heard by all about the seeder,
the jays lambast the card'nal's jarring chime.
"The card'nals songs are dreadful," claims their leader.
"My ears are brought to deafness from their rhyme.
And worst of all their crime of stealing seed,
from us the rightful owners of the feed."

Another bird quite often left forgot,
the feeble sparrows of a feather brown.

By both the jays and card'nals thought of naught,
for sparrow's far too freely pushed around.
Left by the feeder without diddly squat,
the weakly sparrows form a timid sound.
"Please let us eat the seed from feeder's spout,
and spare us from your constant mocking flout."

While sitting, watching birds go battle near,
the seeds have slowly sunk towards feeder's base.
From out the shed Birdkeeper has appeared,
with bag of wicked birdfeed in his brace.
And as he takes a sip of bottled beer,
he walks towards feeder as the birds displace.
Yells, "Son, come help and feed the birds with me,
and after go and water lemon tree."

Annoyed by father's trivial command,
I stand and slowly pace to grab the bag.
I pour the seed into the feeder stand
and think that helping father's such a drag.
After the birds were fed in garden's land,
I trudge towards dry and barren lemon tree.
On turns the faucet for the tree to shower,
as my frustrations for birdkeeper tower.

As sun begins its rest for night's return,
he paints the sky with hues of orange tint.
And at this time the garden birds discern
that sun will radiate his final glint.
They fly to tree for rest in which they yearn
and wait until the sun's proceeding stint.

Replaced by moon, the weaker of the lights,
she wishes garden birds a restful night.

But burrowed in a hole inside a tree,
another bird awakes from daily slumber.
The owl, who rules the night with gift to see
in darkness where the other birds lack number.
Though linked with those who spurn those Christ set free,
like Christ, the owl in darkness bears man's cumber.
Tonight, the owl sets flight to Keeper's place
to tell the truth of feeder to their face.

II

While off in trance by cable news alone,
Birdkeeper sits beside the television.
Instead of making enemies atone,
like feeder, television breeds division.
The folk inside the box of bad news moan
with everlasting cries of foe's derision.
The red and blue presented only sunder
and never grant the viewer thoughts of wonder.

Away from feeder's box of magic spells,
I sit and play some songs on my guitar.
My father yearning evening night to quell,
"Goodnight, dear son; tomorrow isn't far."
And I reply, "Goodnight to you as well."
My father heads to bed beneath the stars,
believed to be alone the rest of night,
oblivious to Owl's approaching flight.

As sleepy eyes made clear night's end was near,
I rose to turn the lights off in the room.
To my surprise outside an owl appears.
Not once I've seen its spotted colored plume.
Its spacious yellow eyes in night see clear.
In awe my own eyes wake and stare in zoom.
Confounded mind unsure of what to do,
to let the owl fly in or make him shoo.

Though hesitant to let him come inside,
the aura owl diffuses captivates.
His radiating glow made me decide,
why not let owl inside the castle gates?
I turned the knob and pulled the door out wide,
while knowing well the mess that birds create.
As owl swooped through the door, I feared disaster.
But owl was calmed within the walls of plaster.

Though unaware of gifts to speak with birds,
I somehow understood the words owl spoke.
"I flew tonight to garden," my ears heard,
"to warn that feeder's seed addicts like coke.
The sweetness of the seed impairs the herds
of all the birds that gather by the oak.
The seeds in feeder makes the mind turn crazy,
and card'nal, jay, and sparrow all grow lazy."

"But how could father's generosity
move birds away from nature's state of being?"
"Birdkeeper, blind to his precocity,
believes the food he gives to birds is freeing.

But feeder just brings animosity.
In fight for feeder's seed birds halt agreeing.
Birdkeeper feeds a toxic world of strife
and hinders birds to live a natural life.

"Another way that feeder pacifies,
it chains the birds addicted to the seed,
preventing birds to venture towards the skies,
tied down to ground enslaved by need for feed.
But what about the birds who skyward rise?
They're never tempted by the feeder's weed.
The birds of flight that glide near heaven's lights,
aren't those the birds that soar to greatest heights?"

"But how come this is so?" I then reply.
"Aren't little birds just bound by nature's chance
to fly near earth instead of soaring high,
like eagles, hawks, and birds of higher stance?"
But owl retorts, "Do card'nals even try
to fly away from garden feeder's trance?
The little birds will only elevate
once they neglect the trick from feeder's bait."

Before the owl flew out the door at last,
he gave the son advice and forward warning.
"The coming days will bear a grim forecast;
impending tribulation some day's morning.
Resulting lively consequences vast,
abiding fear may bring a great aborning.
Remember where your strength and refuge rest;
it lies within the hands of whom thou blest."

As time demanded owl to now depart,
I quietly led owl through our backdoor,
and quickly out the residence owl darts.
Then time to get prepared for bed once more
to sleep, I take the owl's advice to heart,
Debating should I stop the birds from war
though far more troublesome to ease of mind.
What tribulations God will have me find?

III

Upon the heaven's clouds an angel sat
who holds in arms a fiery golden censer.
From God's command his hands release the vat.
The censer drops to earth from God's dispenser.
Through firmament the censer landed flat
upon the ground, provoking God's condenser.
Up high the clouds begin to darken black,
preparing thunderstorms and lightning crack.

Upon the sight above of stormy clouds,
the eagles, crows, and birds of flight depart.
They fly away with flocks of feathered crowds,
to flee to safety 'fore the storm will start.
The card'nals, jays, and sparrows only shroud
beneath the bushes, fearing life may part.
They dare not leave the feeder, so they stay,
too dumb to know that they can fly away.

From gazing up at darkened pitch-black sky,
Birdkeeper spots that thunder clouds are forming.

He runs to me so he could signify:
"Our morning's day is due impending storming."
The Keeper saw the birds that flee from high,
a sign of great severity informing.
What course do keeper and myself decide?
Outrun the storm or lock ourselves inside?

The storm had quickly gained its strength and power.
It ceased sun's daily tenure prematurely.
As light was shunned from day, the depths devour,
with rainfall, winds, and lightning coming surely.
Birdkeeper could not stay another hour;
without the doubt his house would stand securely.
Birdkeeper tells me, "Pack your bags; let's flee
and head due east away from storm at sea."

Then out the door we left with bags in store
and drove ourselves away towards refuge far.
But as we sought to reach an eastward shore,
an even stronger storm surrounds the car.
The clouds begin to darken even more,
as hues of gray bedim as black as char.
This storm had cast a Shadow overhead.
I thought myself, 'tis not the storm I fled.

And from the distance, something faint appeared.
From Shadow's depth, I try discerning it.
As it came near, my vision slowly cleared:
a pale white horse that came from devil's pit.
The horseman swings his sword; through air he sheared.
His long black cloak the whole of his outfit.

The horseman Death arrived for moment's dread
whose presence calls for loss of life ahead.

The pale horse gallops swiftly our direction,
approaching us through gusty winds with speed.
His sword of death creates a clean connection
to Keeper's earthly body. From his stead,
and Death counts one man more for his collection.
Birdkeeper's soul at once from earth was freed.
And there was father fallen, cold and dead;
at foot of stairs the back of head had bled.

Then after Keeper met his mortal end,
both Death and horse left searching other souls.
Some other victim Death will apprehend
and send them straight to purgatory's coals.
Both shocked and full of fear, my thoughts descend
to state of grave despair from life Death stole.
Then after Death had left the area,
the Shadow pushed me towards hysteria.

A jolt of lighting crashes down I hear.
I'm stunned, but quick to grasp the storm's own threat.
And then I am reminded Death's still near;
perhaps he lurks in Shadow's silhouette.
I'll fade away if there's no shelter here;
can't risk my own remains becoming wet.
I quickly find a place for night to rest.
Reflecting day's events, despair congests.

At night storm reached a temporary calm,

though Shadow stayed despite tranquility.
As thoughts of day's events in mind embalmed,
exhaustion gives me immobility.
Regardless of despair from day's own qualms,
at last, I find in sleep stability.
But clear the night shows remnants of the day;
a blood red moon cast over Mobile Bay.

IV

The next day's morning finally arrives,
my first without Birdkeeper by my side.
From yesterday the Shadow still survives,
the raging storm that clearly hasn't died.
The Shadow makes me fear my homebound drive,
for death and horse may still await my ride.
Despaired, in shelter stuck, I'm paralyzed
with no direction yet to be devised.

But suddenly, my mind recalls the owl
who visited back home not long ago.
I could just hide in place like feeder's fowl,
or fly away from danger like the crows.
Forget the lightning strikes and windy howls,
and fight against the rain and gusty blows.
The Shadow's presence makes me want to leave.
Let's travel back to home before the eve.

I step outside beneath the Shadow's cast.
The sharp winds almost sweep me off my feet.
I try to push against the rainy blasts,

but darkened clouds and fearfulness accrete.
Outside I think that I can never last,
so back inside I rush in brisk retreat.
Then at the moment of my greatest test,
I find where my own strength and refuge rest.

Assured by God's unwavering affection,
I sprint outside through Shadow's stormy gusts.
Determined, I push through the strong advection.
A few more steps to reach the car. I must!
I reach the door, step in, and find directions
to travel home through guided Godly trust.
Though as I drive and storm induces swerves,
I lack in fear suppressing anxious nerves.

The further on I drive the more fear wanes.
Persisting through the murky interstate,
my car gets pushed in winds of hurricane.
While leaving Shadow's valley, dark abates;
my heart instantly lifts from Shadow's chains,
with reconning that God controls my fate.
Your rod and staff provide me evil's cures.
Though Shadow has subsided, storm endures.

As I continue moving homeward bound,
I feel the howling winds have speed decrease.
While driving by the Mississippi Sound,
the lightning flashes slowly come to peace.
And once I reach my native stomping grounds,
the storm's downpour has finally deceased.
With storm no longer wreaking reckless harm,

you drove straight through, and now you've found the
    light.
No longer should despair have you feel trapped.
So why should you still flounder time and waste?
While idly sat in dark, your Shadow chased.

"If I could tell you just one crucial thing,
that fear of earthly matters kills your mind.
When mired in fear you miss the truth life brings,
your logos, faith, and intuition blind.
Place trust in God the Father, King of kings.
With reasoning and wonder, truth you'll find.
Remember always whom you love the most,
our God: The Father, Son and Holy Ghost."

As owl's words pause, I ask him what I ponder:
"What do you make of card'nals, jays, and sparrows?"
"By feeder, card'nals moan, and jays just maunder,
and sparrows bow to foreign birds, their pharaohs.
But forced away from feeder they fly yonder,
their spirit elevates from worldview narrow.
The card'nal sings sweet songs, the jays tell jokes,
and sparrow rules their own amongst the oaks."

I comment: "What would happen to the birds
if I refuse to give the feeder seed?"
The owl responds: "The little birds may herd
away from feeder's sweet, addictive weed.
They might try flying heights once thought absurd,
and see the world around like larger breeds.
Perhaps they'll cease their animosity.

You'll never know unless you let them free."

Remembering when Keeper couldn't spot
the eagle in the sky, I then reply:
"One day not long ago, near heaven's lot
I saw an eagle fly across the sky.
I pointed up for dad, but he saw naught
and claimed he could not see the bird. But why?
Were eyes obstructed by his aging vision?
Or maybe that his gaze had lacked precision?"

Owl's answer: "Keeper saw the eagle, too,
so, why'd he claim he saw no bird in air?
Birdkeeper showed the little birds to you,
while knowing you'd find greater birds somewhere.
He hoped the greater birds you would pursue,
but knew that he could never guide you there.
For one's true faith can never be contrived.
Your faith in God must be free-will derived.

"Before I go, I leave one last impression.
Remember this until your dying hour.
The birds of feeder trapped by world's possessions,
those foolish ones deceived by Babel's tower.
But Eagle, strong and noble in expression,
can see the light of God's almighty power.
For you, one question will decide your fate:
What kind of birds will you now emulate?"

The owl flew out the door in shining glow,
and lights the sky he flies through dark of night.

A sudden jolt of new electric flow
illuminates the house as bulbs ignite.
My eyes get weary as exhaustion grows,
so on the couch I rest till morning's light.
When I awake upon tomorrow's dawn,
I must decide which path to travel on.

Though He Slay Me

ANA RATH

PROLOGUE

Dark, mournful clouds streak 'cross a dismal sky.
With zeal, drops beat upon the windowpane.
A man bed-rid hears noise as cars drive by
in lively streets below his grim domain.
His jaded eyes inspect that lonely spot,
for ceiling blemish's all there is to see.
Unfree to move, down, desperate, distraught,
"Have mercy, Lord, and take me now," said he.

"They say I'll be here till I breath my last:
a paralytic in both feet and hands.
My days of useful labor now have passed;
wrung dry am I without the means to stand.
Impediments now bar all kingdom work
I'd planned to offer You and joyf'lly give.
It is enough. Now senseless pains do lurk.

take hands, as each one to the other vows
to have, to hold, from this day till the end.
"I'll be there in the sickness and the health.
I'll love and cherish you with all my heart.
I'll be there in privation and in wealth.
I'll be there till death comes and doth us part."

The sister to the groom from out of town
has traveled far to be here for this day:
her husband minds two girls in white silk gowns,
their daughters and another on the way.
The cripple notes a loving, sideways glance
as Kristy finds the place where nieces stood.
He thinks her happy thoughts could be, perchance,
the longing for a future motherhood.

The messenger now grabbed his arm and said,
"Come now. Let's move away to different scene.
There's more to show you in their years ahead.
Sweet hope and grief and all that lies between."
Nine months have passed since June's sweet wedding bells.
Inside a clinic Drew and Kristy passed.
In faces shined a hope that docs would tell
that treatment would be matter of the past.

Inside the lobby, conversation thrives
from basketball to upcoming exams.
Each wonders how the other one arrives
to a decision on post-bach'lor programs.
At last, a woman dressed in purple scrubs
calls, "Mr. Oldham, follow me this way."

She leads on to a room to take his blood:
a sample that would check for PSA.

The blood was drawn. They waited the result
in white-washed room for doctor would come in,
eager to see what doctor would consult,
now with two years of treatment at an end.
In Easter time when Drew was diagnosed,
"Most treatable," the doctors had assured.
But doctor's news now quickly dashed their hopes:
"The cancer's back. Recov'y's not secure."

II

"Let us move now to different scene," led he.
Immediately, the office fled from sight.
They found themselves in company of three:
the couple and a woman of insight.
Her hair was gray, and wrinkles lined her face;
yet underneath her features wisdom flowed.
Her eyes were deep and full of gentle grace
of one who long had walked the narrow road.

The cripple stares at what here lies ahead:
a room in modest home whose walls were filled
with saturated shelves of books well read
and potted-plants upon each window sill.
They sit with folded hands and eyes downcast.
The cripple hears the name of God invoked.
"What is this place?" he to companion asked.
He gestured, "Julie—friend to Andy's folks."

"They seek assurance that this illness show
no deep or hidden fault on either part.
As Job does prove, it is not always so.
Nevertheless it is a place to start.
Through guided pray'r, they ask the Lord to search
and know their hearts and see if grievous way
be found in them, that they may in this church
confess and be restored to health one day."

The paralytic looks again upon
three friends as they God's presence gravely sought.
Then of the sudden, Kristy, calmness gone,
looked up with startled look of novel thought.
She turned and said, "It came to me just now
a feeling that I wanted desperately—
(it came so clear as if one spoke aloud)—
to be with child and have a family."

Surprise did not appear in Julie's tone.
She was familiar with the way God speaks;
she knew He seldom speaks in megaphone,
though He's not far from those who truly seek.
"Alright, now let us lift this up in prayer."
She took their hands and bowed her head and said,
"God, what do You intend now for this pair?
What plan have You in time when healing spreads?"

A perfect silence over all three loomed.
Their watchful expectation one could sense.
The cripple felt a presence fill the room;
he trembled then in awe and fear intense.

His guide divine said, "Do not be afraid.
I've asked that God would open now your eyes,
that you may see how God to all who've prayed
employs us in response to their deep cries."

At this, he touched the paralytic's eye.
A radiant light illuminates the place.
He makes out figure, bright as noonday sky,
possessing a familiar, holy face.
The lame man saw the hallowed figure bend
in front of praying couple on divan.
He whispered soft, and soul did comprehend,
though words were spoke in language not of man.

"I came to them," the bright companion sung,
"I told them all I'd been instructed to.
Though spoke I not in words of human tongue,
they understood what God was going to do.
I told them that the Lord had heard them grieve.
I told them He would grant this deepest feeling.
I told them Kristy would a son conceive,
that he would be a sign of Andy's healing."

III

The scene of praying man and wife now clears.
The messenger guides on to other space.
"The cancer has been on and off for years.
A hiatus for three months has taken place.
They sense the time is now to have a child,
yet now it seems less certain Drew will stay.

they broke the news to fam'ly lovéd thus:
the card to introduce their "Baby O"
read "Merry Christmas from the THREE of Us."

IV

When vision closed, another one came in:
another doctor's office, white and strange.
The couple sat before them, faces grim.
The doubting cripple saw at once the change.
The youthful jokester of the wedding morn
now jaded looked at suffering prolonged:
a war-torn body, weariéd and worn,
though eyes still clear revealed a spirit strong.

"He's fading fast, and right before my eyes,"
said man who's crippled in more ways than one.
"like summer grass beneath the windy skies,
that's here today, but gone tomorrow morn."
Companion pined, "And He who feeds the birds
and knows the day and place that each one falls,
much more He sees the pain and hears the words
that here takes place from His gold, heav'nly halls."

"When you first came our way, I must confess,"
began the smart oncologist to say,
"I did not think your case would cause such stress.
There seemed great hope to keep disease at bay.
We surgically removed the tumors' head.
We cleared your neck and chest from cancerous growth.
The chemo seemed to limit well the spread

of cancer spots, the old and new ones both."

The doctor paused. A quick glance showed the strife
endured by his young patient, frail and gaunt,
and so as well by his most pregnant wife.
"We can keep trying, if that's what you want.
If you both want to not give up the fight,
perhaps I can dream up some cocktail new.
I must here warn that chance is only slight
at this point of us getting this for you."

His voice lapsed off. And silence filled the room.
The clock ticked on while minutes seemed to crawl.
The cripple shivered, as if death-cold tomb
had replaced the office's clean, white-washed walls.
Slow moments passed. Then Kristy caught Drew's eye.
The cripple saw at once they thought as one.
The treatment road—its lows and fleeting highs—
must finish and be altogether done.

The companion said what cripple had deduced:
"Six years of treatment 'pon Drew's frame did weigh.
No walking, hiking, fishing could he do;
the cancer'd taken all of that away.
She'd married once an athlete, strong and tall.
Yet after sessions now, he'd need her aid
to reach their own front door, lest he should fall.
Exhaustion total he could not evade.

"They'd had enough. Fight on they could no more.
They chose this risky path without remorse:

the Lord himself must either heal him, or
disease would be allowed to run its course.
The doctor Drew then asked, "How long have I?"
in a shadow of a voice that once was strong.
A momentary pause, then came reply:
"I cannot say for sure. It won't be long."

This declaration hit them all like lead.
Soon tears poured down Drew's face as from a cup.
He turned to Kristy, pregnant wife, and said:
"I wish I could have watched our boy grow up."
Companion turned: "I'd watched close over Drew
since he was still a boy-child not yea high.
Come rain, come shine, come life in any hue,
this was the first I'd ever seen him cry."

V

The scene then closed as if by misty veils.
The crippled one could not contain a yell:
"Why come you here to tell depressing tales?
I get the inkling that this won't end well."
"End well?" paused he sent down from God above.
"Does not the Cross convince you that it will?
Has God not proved there His unfailing love?
Though pain be great, His love runs deeper still."

The cripple stopped at angel's stern reproof.
His eyes diverted from companion's gaze.
"God watches Andy die, yet stands aloof.
But surely He is great and strong to save."

"I know not why God lets some suffer so.
But know I that His own Son was not spared.
Such love as this must surely trust bestow.
He's working all things out for good," he shared.

The cripple lifted eyes and looked around:
before them, couch on which the sick man lay.
Outside, the sky unleashes deaf'ning sound,
and open windows let in pounding spray.
Before the couch which bed-rid Andy used,
his hopeful and expectant wife did kneel.
"I wonder what it looks like," Kristy mused,
"to see the Lord miraculously heal."

"To understand, I must here make it plain:
there is a song that Kristy loved to play.
The lyrics spoke of God's clean, 'Healing Rain.'
She waited now, expectant for the day
when God would send the promised healing storm.
With mercy raining down, she could be sure:
the torrent strong would cleanse, and on the morn,
belovéd Drew would be completely cured.

"There came two storms of fierce and fiery might
within the last weeks of his hospice care.
Both times she woke and waited for the sight
when God would heal in answer to her prayer.
Let us now jump to night of darkness deep.
Drew woke and tried to tell his Kristy something.
Speech faint and slurred, she lulled him back to sleep.
His last attempt to speak amounted nothing.

"Regrettably, I've not been apt to make
some sense when spoke Drew of some Narnian strife.
But from that sleep no more would Andy wake."
Soon Kristy saw from him no signs of life.
Not she nor those around desired talk.
At last, dawn graced the deathly room with light.
Her dad, come in from early morning walk,
said, "Sidewalk's wet. It must have rained last night."

She glanced up at her father, eyes aglow,
as stunning realization became clear.
She touched Drew's ashen cheek, as fresh tears flow.
"God did send healing rain for you, Drew dear.
It came not when all heaven's might was stirred
to beat with sound and fury 'pon the pane.
It came so still, so small it passed unheard.
He took you home. He healed in quiet rain."

Companion picked up story to say more:
"She worried as Drew's birthday fast approached;
yet as it were, the child came day before.
Her mind elsewhere, her grief could not be broached."
Her boy she cradled in her arms and smiled,
"Though sight I lack, the Lord I've put my faith in.
He's graced me with this precious, promised child.
A gift of God, I name my firstborn Nathan."

EPILOGUE

"The steadfast Drew and Kristy, tried by fire,
recall another tale," the angel spoke.

"Three friends were given ultimatum dire:
to worship golden statue or be smoked.
Spoke they, 'O King, we serve a God whose name
is mighty and will save us from your hand.
But even if He has not so ordained,
we will not bend our knee to form of man.'

"If Shadrack, Meshach, and Abednego,
though facing fiery furnace, bravely stood,
how much can you and story's couple know
God's working all these moments out for good?
Your faith in God is not on shaky ground;
you need not make some mad leap in the dark.
This side of heav'n, questions may abound
but God has proved His love," the guide remarked.

"As Drew once said, so it did come to pass.
For time did heal, though scar there'd always be.
The God of comfort sent me down at last
to once again plant words of hopeful seed.
I told her that when I Drew's soul did bear
to golden gates to join the heav'nly chant,
she greeted Drew—a girl with curly hair,
the second zygote never to implant."

The cripple thought again to portrait hall:
there Drew had cradled in his arms the girl.
That look of love and trust he could recall.
God'd given wife a son and man a pearl.
The paralyzed looked 'pon his crippled form.
"Since it be so that God, His Son not sparing,

so proved his love, now praise shall be my norm!
I'll trust Him still, no matter how I'm faring."

Rain clouds still spanned across the morning sky.
Their drops still fell upon the windowpane.
Conditions, though, that once were cause to sigh
no longer threatened peace of his domain.
The lesson given had not been for naught:
"You've freed my crippled soul, and now I see.
O Abba God, how mercif'lly You've taught:
You're here, though I with crippled body be."

Endnotes

INTRODUCTION

1. Syllabus available on my academic homepage: https://home.uchicago.edu/~rfulton/Writing%20Christian%20Poetry.pdf. For my blog, go to https://fencingbearatprayer.blogspot.com. Visit https://dragoncommonroom.com for our long-form narratives *Aurora Bearialis, Centrism Games,* and *Draco Alchemicus.*

2. John Martineau, *Trivium: The Classical Liberal Arts of Grammar, Logic, & Rhetoric* (New York: Bloomsbury, 2016); Ernst Robert Curtius, *European Literature and the Latin Middle Ages,* trans. Willard R. Trask (Princeton: Princeton University Press, 1953, 2013); Anthony Esolen, *Ironies of Faith: The Laughter at the Heart of Christian Literature* (Wilmington, Delaware: 2007); Malcolm Guite, *Faith, Hope and Poetry: Theology and the Poetic Imagination* (New York: Routledge, 2012); and Andrew Thornton-Norris, *The Spiritual History of English* (The Social Affairs Unit, 2009).

3. Tolkien, "Mythopoeia," in *Tree and Leaf* (London: HarperCollins, 2001), 88.

4. Curtius, *European Literature,* trans. Trask, 145-54.

5. "Caedmon's Hymn," trans. Craig Williamson, *The Complete Old English Poems* (Philadelphia: University of Pennsylvania Press, 2017), 1050.

6. Bede, *The Ecclesiastical History of the English People,* iv.24(22), trans. Bertram Colgrave, ed. Judith McClure and Roger Collins (Oxford: Oxford University Press, 1994), 215-17.

7. For introduction to these authors and lists of their narrative retellings of the Scriptures, see Willemien Otten and Karla Pollman, eds., *Poetry and Exegesis in Premodern Latin Christianity: The Encounter between Classical and Christian Strategies of Interpretation* (Leiden: Brill, 2007).

8. The comparison is less fanciful than it may seem. See Richard Keller Simon, "*Star Wars* and *The Faerie Queene,*" in *Trash Culture: Popular Culture and the Great Tradition* (Berkeley and Los Angeles: University of California Press, 1999), 29-37, for Lucas's dependence on the Elizabethan poet Edmund Spenser's mythical allegory, *The Faerie Queene.*

9. *The Little Office of the Blessed Virgin Mary and The Office of the Dead. In Latin and English* (Kansas City, Missouri: Angelus Press, 2014), 8-9. For the importance of the Office for medieval Christians, see Rachel Fulton Brown, *Mary and the Art of Prayer: The Hours of the Virgin in Medieval Christian Life and Thought* (New York: Columbia University Press, 2017).

10. Esolen, *Ironies of Faith*, 322.

11. Tolkien, "Mythopoeia," in *Tree and Leaf*, 87.

12. Augustine, *On Music*, 6.11 (29), trans. Robert Catesby Taliaferro, in *The Fathers of the Church* 4 (Washington, D.C.: The Catholic University of America Press, 1947), 355.

13. Guite, *Faith, Hope and Poetry*, 23.

14. Tolken, "On Fairy-Stories," in *Tree and Leaf*, 72.

15. Esolen, *Ironies of Faith*, 58.

16. Esolen, *Ironies of Faith*, 58.

17. Tolkien, "On Fairy-Stories," in *Tree and Leaf*, 70.

18. Tolkien, *The Lord of the Rings*, 6.IV (Boston: Houghton Mifflin, 2004), 954.

19. Thornton-Norris, *Spiritual History*, 148.

20. See the introductions to the respective Arts in Martianus Capella, *The Marriage of Mercury and Philology*, trans. William Harris Stahl with E. L. Budge (New York: Columbia University Press, 1992).

21. Tolkien, "Mythopoeia," in *Tree and Leaf*, 87: "The heart of man is not compound of lies, / but draws some wisdom from the only Wise, / and still recalls him."

22. Tolkien, "Mythopoeia," in *Tree and Leaf*, 89: "I would with the beleaguered fools be told, / that keep an inner fastness where their gold, / impure and scanty, yet they loyally bring, / to mint in image of distant king / .... I will not walk with your progressive apes, / erect and sapient."

23. Gerard Manley Hopkins, "Pied Beauty," in *Moral Beauty, God's Grace: Major Poems and Spiritual Writings*, ed. John F. Thornton and Susan B. Varenne (New York: Vintage Books, 2003), 25.

24. Hopkins, "Pied Beauty," in *Moral Beauty*, 25.

25. Tolkien, *Letters*, ed. Humphrey Carpenter (Boston: Houghton Mifflin, 1995), 214, 221.

26. Tolkien, "On Fairy-Stories, in *Tree and Leaf*, 22.

27. Anthony Esolen, *The Hundredfold: Songs for the Lord* (San Francisco: Ignatius Press, 2019), 44; Tolkien, "On Fairy-Stories," in *Tree and Leaf*, 33-46.

28. Tolkien, "On Fairy-Stories," in *Tree and Leaf*, 73.

29. Tolkien, "Mythopoeia," in *Tree and Leaf*, 90.

Rachel Fulton Brown

Rachel Fulton Brown is Associate Professor of History at the University of Chicago, where she teaches courses on the history of Christianity, medieval European religious, cultural, and intellectual history, and the works of J.R.R. Tolkien. She is the author of *From Judgment to Passion: Devotion to Christ and the Virgin Mary, 800-1200* (2002), and *Mary and the Art of Prayer: The Hours of the Virgin in Medieval Christian Life and Thought* (2017), and she has held fellowships from the Guggenheim Foundation, the Mellon Foundation, the American Council of Learned Societies, and the National Humanities Center, among others. In her public life, she blogs as *Fencing Bear at Prayer*, and she lectures on Logos, Tolkien, and medieval history at Unauthorized.tv. The Dragon Common Room is her online forum for training poets in the arts of the Christian imagination. She livestreams weekly on *The Mosaic Ark*, where she and co-host Kilts Khalfan will take you on a nautical journey through the mythology and symbolism of the Internet.

By the Same Author

From Judgment to Passion: Devotion to Christ and the Virgin Mary, 800–1200

Mary and the Art of Prayer: The Hours of the Virgin in Medieval Christian Life and Thought

Milo Chronicles: Devotions 2016 - 2019

AS EDITOR

History in the Comic Mode: Medieval Communities and the Matter of Person

Centrism Games: A Modern Dunciad

Aurora Bearialis

FORTHCOMING

Draco Alchemicus

9 7 9 8 2 1 8 2 5 3 6 0 8